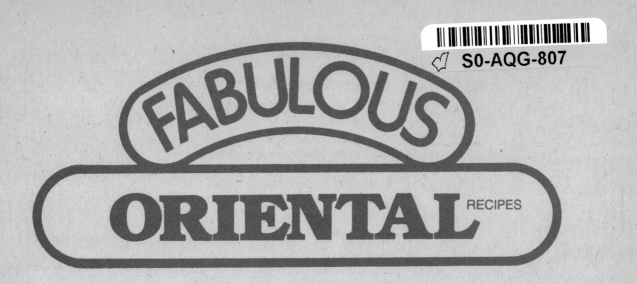

FABULOUS ORIENTAL RECIPES

by

Johna Blinn

Edited by
Tom Dorsey

PUBLISHED BY PLAYMORE INC., PUBLISHERS AND WALDMAN PUBLISHING CORP.
New York, New York
Printed in Canada/Cover Printed in USA

Fabulous Cookbook Series
Prepared Under the Editorial Direction of
Malvina G. Vogel

Illustrated by Arthur Friedman

Designed by Irva Mandelbaum

Cover photo: Twice-Fried Pork with Ginger Sauce
Courtesy of Argo/Kingsford's Corn Starch

Acknowledgment

The author is indebted to the following for assistance in making this a useful cookbook: Claire Boasi, Ruth Lundgren, Caryl Saunders, Anita Fial, Chris Pines, Virginia Schroeder, Rae Hartfield, Yvonne Martin, Ina Balin, Pat Mason, Kay Murphy O'Flynn, Eileen Edwards Denne, Dodie Sway, Marlys Bielunski, George Burke, Beryl Walter, Jeanne M. Bauer, Ray L. Clark, Roxie Howlett, Sally Brunot, Doris Koch, Donna Higgins, Donna Hamilton, Margaret Spader, Frances Fleming, Patricia O'Keefe, Wade Whitfield, Eileen Jaynes, Elaine T. Beatson, Dee Munson, Kay Engelhardt, Morgan Nitzberg, Barbara Tomorowitz, Alice Gautsch, Benji Taechanarong, MarJeanne Bell, Valerie Itkin, Jean Howard, Gloria Marshall, Carole Georgeas, Ann Norman, Kathryn Zeluck, Beth Anderson, Charlene Kirchheimer, Lois Westlund, Mrs. H. Tarumato, National Livestock & Meat Board, Georgia/Alabama Peanut Growers, California Dried Fig Advisory Board, Ocean Garden Products, Inc., American Spice Trade Association, Angostura International Limited, Tea Council of the USA, Inc., Campbell Soup Co., New Jersey Asparagus Industry Council, Standard Brands, Inc., American Egg Board, Best Foods, Rice Council, California Almond Growers Exchange, National Duckling Council, Diamond Walnut Growers, Inc., Castle & Cooke Foods (Dole, Bumble Bee), General Foods (Birdseye, Minute Rice), Del Monte Kitchens, Sunkist Growers, Inc., American Lamb Council, California Iceberg Lettuce Commission, National Fisheries Institute, Inc., Lawry Foods, Inc., Kikkoman International Inc., Florida Citrus Commission, United Fresh Fruits and Vegetables Commission, Tuna Research Foundation, McIlhenny Company, Tuna Research Foundation, Banana Bunch, New Zealand Lamb, Inc., Calavo Growers of America, American Mushrooms Institute, Lea & Perrins Worcestershire Sauce, Wild Rice Council, Florida Celery Exchange, La Choy Food Products (Division of Beatrice Foods Co.), Chun King Foods, California Advisory Board, Argo/Kingsford's Corn Starch, Japan National Tourist Organization, Bangkok No. 2 Restaurant (Los Angeles), J.M. Smucker Co., National Pork Producers Council, The Fresh Garlic Association, South African Rock Lobster Service Corporation, H.J. Heinz Co., International Multifoods (Ketshchmer Wheat Germ), Alaska Seafood Marketing Institute, Planter's Oil Test Kitchen, Standard Brands, Inc., Karo Corn Syrup, Mazola Corn Oil, Pasadena Buddhist Women's Association, and Jeanette Cheng.

J.B.

BARONET
B·O·O·K·S

BARONET BOOKS is a trademark of Playmore Inc., Publishers
and Waldman Publishing Corp., New York, N.Y.

The Author

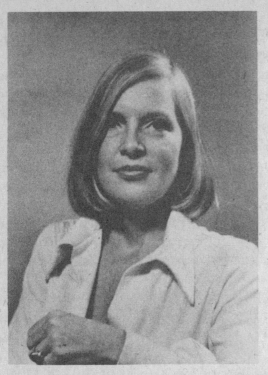

To many of the top movie and television stars, Johna Blinn is a celebrity. For almost 20 years they have welcomed her into their homes, onto sets, just about anywhere to talk about food, entertaining and lifestyles. Her column, "Celebrity Cookbook," is syndicated throughout the world and appears weekly in more than 140 newspapers and periodicals. A collection of hundreds of these conversations and recipes appears in *Celebrity Cookbook* published by Waldman Publishing Corporation.

Blinn is a former assistant food editor of LOOK magazine and is the author of a number of books, including *The Shangri-la Cookbook*. While she is busy working on her first novel and screenplay, Blinn still manages to serve as a frequent contributor of indepth interviews, profiles and entertainment features to newspapers and magazines in the U. S. and abroad.

A graduate of the State University of Iowa, Blinn took graduate work in home economics at the University of Wisconsin and taught home economics in Iowa, Virginia and New York. Now based in Los Angeles, she is married to a nationally-known newspaper syndicate editor, writer and management consultant, and they have two teenage children.

Introduction

This is a guide to Oriental gustatory pleasures that can be easily prepared in your own kitchen. Far-eastern simple, off-beat recipes for appetizers, main dishes, vegetables and sweets — culled from favorite court dishes of ancient Chinese emperors, rice tables of Indian and Indonesian princes, Tibetian nomads, Vietnamese refugees, Korean and Japanese fishermen and organic food lovers. And all are adapted for easy, at-home presentations.

In this cookbook, we are trying to satisfy your craving for Chinese, Japanese and other foods of the Orient, sure, but we also hope to remove you from fast food to taste treats that are worth waiting for, not simply a matter of 10 minutes in the oven. The Orient is an appropriate theme, for it is a place of quiet pleasure, a place where, for over a thousand years, good food and dining have been elevated to a special place of honor and reverence.

Great care is taken not only in the selection and preparation of Oriental food, but in its presentation. The Japanese particularly stress the esthetics of the food and strive to prepare a feast for the eye and mind as well as the stomach. The actual physical setting for formal dining is very important. The elaborate tea ceremony or formal dinner party is held, if possible, in quiet, serene surroundings, like a garden.

Cooking Oriental implies putting into practice some of these principles: Like the great Chinese cooks, you can, with a little ingenuity and practice, create an infinite variety of dishes using the same staples, cutting food with a Chinese cleaver prior to cooking rather than slicing later (as done in the Western manner), and improving timing so vegetables are crisp and tender in stir-fry dishes. You will soon learn how to marinate or flavor food to give it a subtlety or pungency by the use of sauces or spices. These are only a few of the tricks that can turn the most banal foods into ambrosias, to create memorable foods for yourself and your family.

The result we hope we have achieved in these pages is a constellation of Oriental recipes gleaned by ignoring all time or geographical barriers: from ancient Chinese emperors' favorites to the more elaborate offerings from the rice table and special menus of all modern Oriental cultures.

Foreign or hard-to-get ingredients have been kept to a minimum. However, when they are used, you are told where to obtain them or given substitutes. To keep the cook happy and serene, recipes have deliberately been kept short, simple and healthy, using as many fresh foods as possible.

In addition to the hundreds of recipes in this book, we would like to add one more, provided by a group of women who helped us with some of the authentic Japanese delicacies: the Pasadena Buddhist Women's Association:

HAPPY HOME RECIPE
Serves all

4 cups Love	5 cups Understanding
2 cups Loyalty	3 cups Forgiveness
5 quarts Faith	1 cup Friendship
2 tablespoons Tenderness	5 teaspoons Hope
1 cup Kindness	1 barrel Laughter

Take LOVE and LOYALTY; mix thoroughly with FAITH. Blend with TENDERNESS, KINDNESS, UNDERSTANDING and FORGIVENESS. Add FRIENDSHIP and HOPE; sprinkle abundantly with LAUGHTER. Bake with SUNSHINE. Serve daily with generous helpings.

J.B.

CONTENTS

APPETIZERS

Chicken Nibblers with Sauce 7
Mandarin Chicken-Iceberg Packets 7
Plum Blossom Chicken Wings 8
Shrimp Kabuki with Dipping Sauce 8
Sesame Seed Chicken Bits 9
Sweet & Sour Chicken Wings 9
Teriyaki Chicken Wings 9
Chicken Tempura with Dipping Sauces 10
Crabmeat Won Tons 11
Fried Shrimp Toast 11
Japanese Crab Tidbits 12
Shrimp with Sweet & Sour Sauce 12
Seafood or Chicken Tempura with
    Tempura Sauce 13
Cantonese Meatballs with Orange Teriyaki Dip . . 14
Rumaki 14
Chinese Pineapple Meatballs 15
Marinated Mushrooms 15
Indonesian Beef Sate 16
Marinated Steak Appetizers 16
Egg Rolls (Chinese Crêpes) 17
Pork Satay Singapore 17
Orange-Teriyaki Ribs, Microwaved 18
Samosas 18
Char Siu 19
Fried Rice Rolls 19

SOUPS

Bombay Curried Banana Chicken Chowder 20
Chinese Rice Soup 20
Japanese Chicken Soup with Noodles 20
Cantonese Sweet & Sour Soup 21
Egg Drop Soup 21
Lotus Soup 21
Oyster Stew Orientale 22
Sweet & Sour Chicken Soup Salmagundi 22
Korean Wedding Beef Soup with Meatballs 23

SALADS

Bombay Chicken Salad 24
Chinese Almond Rice Salad with Soy Dressing . . 24
Chang's Cucumber Salad 25
Chinese Chicken Salad Le Grand Buffet
    with Dijon Sherry Dressing 25
Far-East Spinach Salad 26
Teriyaki Salad 26
Indonesian Vegetable Salad with
    Peanut Dressing 27
Jade Tree Iceberg Salad 27
Cantonese Walnut Lobster Salad with
    Sweet & Sour Dressing 28
Asian Vegetable Salad with
    Ginger Soy Dressing 29
Marinated Celery & Shrimp Salad 29
Gourmet Beef Salad 30
Honey Banana Salad 30

SALADS (cont.)

Tuna Chinese Almond Salad 30
Dragon Whiskers Salad 31
Korean Eggplant Salad 31

POULTRY

Almond Chicken, Chow Style 32
Chicken Cashew 32
Angostura Oriental Chicken 33
Chinese Smoked Chicken in Bag 33
Banana & Chicken Stir-Fry 34
Sweet 'n' Sour Chicken 34
Chicken & Vegetables Oriental 35
Chinese Chicken with Peanuts 35
Chicken Chan 36
Chicken Tandoori with Spiced Tomato Sauce . . . 36
Chicken Chinois 37
Emperor's Chicken Suey 37
Easy Walnut Chicken Stir-Fry 38
Festive Chinese Chicken 38
Himalayan Chicken Curry with Rice 39
Sambal Goreng (Spiced Chicken
    with Vegetables) 39
Ground Turkey Taipei 40
Hop Po Gai Ding (Chicken with Walnuts) 40
Imperial Chicken Suey 41
Sherried Chinese Chicken Casserole 41
Moo Goo Gai Pan 42
Holiday Duckling Stuffed with Apricots 43
Teriyaki Barbecued Chicken 43
Chinese Chunks of Duckling with
    Canton Sauce 44
Turkey Oriental 44

FISH & SEAFOOD

Chu's Dragon Fish with Sweet & Sour Sauce . . . 45
Crab & Vegetables Mikado 45
Floundering Cakes 46
Halibut Hong Kong 46
Japanese Scallops in Sake 46
Lobster with Black Bean Sauce 47
Shrimp Chow Mein 47
Rainbow Trout with Chinese Black Bean Sauce . . 48
Shrimp Curry 48
Shrimp Canton 49
Sweet & Pungent Shrimp 49
Shrimp Vindaloo 50
Fried Rock Lobster with Subgum Sauce 50
Mandarin Sweet 'n' Sour Rock Lobster
    with Pineapple 51
Singing Fish Stew 51
Rock Lobster Chow Mein 52
Taka-Yaki, House of Sue Ouchi
    (Crab-Tofu Omelet) 52
Rock Lobster Kyoto 53
Stir-Fried Rock Lobster, House of Liu 53
Salmon Teriyaki 53
Gingered Shrimp Oriental 54
Saucy Shrimp Cantonese 54

BEEF

Beef with Peppers & Tomatoes 55
Eggplant with Spicy Beef, House of Len 55
Cantonese Grilled Steak with Oyster Sauce 56
Japanese Beef & Noodle Stew 56
Korean-Style Short Ribs 56
Lion's Heads. 57
Sukiyaki Kyoto 57
Beef Sukiyaki 58
Sirloin Steak Nectarine Sukiyaki 58
Cantonese Beef 59
Mikado's Beef with Broccoli Buds 59
Beef Teriyaki with Variations &
 Quick Sweet & Sour Sauce 60
Meatball Chop Suey 61
Stir-Fried Gingered Beef 61
Imperial Beef 62
Mandarin Beef with Almond Rice 62
Emir's Beef Curry 63
Junk Meatballs Cantonese. 63
Plum Wonderful Steak Kabobs 64
Steak-on-a-Stake 64

LAMB

Curried Lamb with Bananas 65
Gingered Lamb & Vegetables Orientale 65
Limed Lamb Shreds with Rice 66
Yushan-Style Spring Lamb 66

PORK

Banana Sweet & Sour Pork. 67
Cantonese Pork Steak Strips 67
Chinese Pork Shoulder Steaks 68
Far-Eastern Butterfly Pork Chops 68
Chow Mein Noodle-Pork Vegetable Medley . . . 69
Braised Ginger Pork 70
Hunan Pork 70
Orange Sausage Bundles 71
Pork Sate with Peanut Sauce. 71
Imperial Pork Loin 72
Pork Chop Suey 72
Pork Chow Mein 73
Stir-Fry Pork with Almonds 73
Pork Lo Mein 74
Sweet & Sour Spareribs 74
Fukien Pork & Tomatoes 75
Tim Suen Yoke (Sweet & Sour Pork) 75
Jou Ssu Pai Ts ' Ai (Cabbage & Meat Shreds) . . . 76
Pineapple-Marinated Spareribs 76
Spareribs Orientale 76
Cantonese Pork Dinner 77
Heavenly Pork with Choy Sum 77

RICE PLUS NOODLES

Browned Rice with Cashews 78
Currant Rice 78
Na Meshi (Green Rice) 78
Apricot-Ginger Oriental Rice 79
Fried Bacon Rice. 79
Ham Fried Rice. 79
Jade Noodles 80
Peanut-Brown Rice Oriental 80

EGGS

Curried Eggs. 81
Egg Foo Yung Pancakes with Hot Soyed Sauce . . 81
Fried Rice Quiche 82
Oriental Eggs Supreme 82
Egg Foo Yung with Chinese Brewa Gravy 83
Haw Jing Tau Tha (Egg-Shrimp Scramble) 83
Cha Tom (Indo-China Pork-Seafood Omelet) . . 84
Lobster Omelet 84
Salmon Foo Yung with Clear Sauce 85
Siamese Stuffed Omelet 85

VEGETABLES & VEGETARIAN

Bok Choy, Bamboo Shoots & Mushrooms 86
Green Beans Mandarin 86
Oriental Celery-Mushroom Sauté 86
Carrots de Chine. 87
Chinese Cauliflower with Almonds 87
Sweet & Sour Beets with Toasted Almonds 87
Microwaved Celery & Peppers, Chinese Style . . . 88
Stir-Fried Chinese Cabbage. 88
Stir-Fried Chinese Pea Pods with
 Water Chestnuts 88
Chinese Vegetables. 89
Curried Eggplant Raita 89
Vegetarian Sukiyaki 89
Curried Vegetable Melange 90
Zen Vegetarian Loaf 90

DESSERTS

Chinese Pineapple Steamed Sponge Cake 91
Fresh Fruit & Lychee Compote 91
Ceylonese Love Cake 92
Pineapple Rice Pudding 92
Chinese Almond Cookies 93
Oriental Almond Rice Cookies 93
Honey Almond Pears 93
Korean Date Balls 94
Peking Dust 94
Banana Fritters 95
Cantonese Apricot Bars 95
Apricot Shangri-la Pudding 96
Chinese Fried Pastries with Walnut Filling 96

Chicken Nibblers with Sauce

Makes 24 appetizers

1 boneless chicken breast (1 pound)
1 teaspoon salt
2 tablespoons sake
¼ cup rice wine vinegar

2½ tablespoons soy sauce
3 teaspoons sugar
1½ teaspoons prepared yellow mustard
thin crackers or wafers

1. Rub chicken with salt; sprinkle with sake.
2. Place chicken in steamer over boiling water; cook 20 minutes, or until tender.
3. Set aside to cool.
4. Cut into bite-size pieces and spear on cocktail picks.
5. Serve with sauce made by combining vinegar, soy sauce, sugar and mustard; serve thin crackers or wafers on the side.

Mandarin Chicken-Iceberg Packets

Serves 10 to 12 (or 3½ to 4 cups filling for lettuce cups)

1 large head iceberg lettuce
2 whole chicken breasts
(about 2 pounds)
3 tablespoons soy sauce
1 can (8 ounces) water chestnuts

1 cup celery, chopped
1 cup fresh mushrooms, chopped
½ cup scallions, chopped
2 tablespoons corn oil
Mandarin Sauce

lemon wedges (optional)

1. Select a loose head of iceberg lettuce. Core, rinse and thoroughly drain lettuce; chill in plastic crisper or disposable plastic bag.
2. Remove skin and bones from chicken; chop meat finely.
3. Combine chicken with soy sauce; refrigerate 15 minutes, or longer.
4. Meanwhile, drain and chop water chestnuts; chop remaining vegetables.
5. Combine ingredients for Mandarin Sauce; set aside.
6. Heat oil in 10-inch skillet; add chicken and stir-fry over high heat until chicken is cooked through.
7. Add vegetables and continue stir-frying about 2 minutes.
8. Add Mandarin Sauce mixture and cook over high heat, stirring until liquid is reduced and thickened. (Vegetables should have just a light coating of thick sauce which binds mixture together.) Remove from heat; chill.
9. Carefully separate leaves of lettuce and arrange in serving bowl; serve chicken mixture in separate bowl, letting guests spoon it into leaves.
10. Serve with lemon wedges, if desired.

Mandarin Sauce

½ cup hot water
1 chicken bouillon cube
2 teaspoons chili powder
1½ teaspoons cornstarch

1½ teaspoons fresh ginger, chopped
1 large clove garlic, minced
(¾ teaspoon)
½ teaspoon salt

½ teaspoon dry mustard

Combine all ingredients and follow above directions.

Plum Blossom Chicken Wings

Serves 15

3 pounds chicken wings
2 tablespoons peanut oil
½ teaspoon salt
dash pepper
1 small onion, peeled and minced

⅔ cup plum jam
¼ cup port wine
1 tablespoon soy sauce
1½ teaspoons fresh lemon juice
1½ teaspoons Dijon mustard

1 can (8 ounces) crushed pineapple in juice

1. Cut chicken wings into 3 pieces at joints. (Reserve wing tips for stock.)
2. Heat oil in wok over high heat; add chicken and season with salt and pepper.
3. Cook, turning occasionally, until golden brown, about 20 minutes.
4. Drain off all pan drippings. Add onion and sauté until tender.
5. Stir in remaining ingredients; bring to a boil and cook about 5 minutes, or until jam is melted and sauce coats chicken.
6. Serve warm as appetizer or spoon over rice for entree.

Shrimp Kabuki with Dipping Sauce

Serves 4 to 6

1 pound raw shrimp, approximately 24
1 cup unsifted flour
1 teaspoon baking powder
1 teaspoon salt

2 eggs
½ cup milk
peanut oil
Dipping Sauce

1. Peel shrimp and split in butterfly fashion, leaving tails on; devein.
2. In a large bowl, blend flour, baking powder and salt.
3. Combine eggs, milk and ½ tablespoon peanut oil; add to dry ingredients. Beat with egg beater until smooth.
4. Fold shrimp into batter.
5. Remove shrimp from batter; fry in peanut oil heated to 375° F. until golden brown.
6. Serve shrimp with Dipping Sauce.

Dipping Sauce

½ cup onion, chopped
1 large clove garlic, minced
2 tablespoons peanut oil
½ cup soy sauce
⅓ cup water

¼ cup dry red wine
2 tablespoons sugar
1 tablespoon cornstarch
¼ teaspoon ground ginger

1. Cook onion and garlic in peanut oil in a small saucepan until onion is tender.
2. Add soy sauce, water, wine, sugar, cornstarch and ginger; heat, stirring until thickened.
3. Cook over low heat 5 minutes, stirring occasionally.

Sesame Seed Chicken Bits

Makes about 24 hors d'oeuvres

⅓ cup dry sherry (or sake)
⅓ cup salad (or sesame) oil
¼ cup imported soy sauce
½ teaspoon ground ginger

¼ teaspoon garlic powder
2 chicken breasts, skinned,
  boned and split
⅓ cup toasted sesame seed*

1. In medium bowl, combine sherry, oil, soy sauce, ginger and garlic powder.
2. Cut each half of chicken breast into 6 pieces (makes about 24 pieces); add to spiced sherry mixture, stirring well. Cover and refrigerate 2 to 3 hours.
3. Broil under preheated moderate broiler (375° F.) for 6 to 8 minutes on each side.
4. Sprinkle with toasted sesame seed; serve with toothpicks.

*To toast sesame seed: sprinkle evenly in jelly-roll pan and bake at 375° F. for 6 to 8 minutes, or until browned.

Sweet & Sour Chicken Wings

Makes 12 appetizers

2 pounds chicken wings
corn oil
½ cup vinegar
½ cup water
½ cup catsup

½ cup sugar
salt to taste
1 teaspoon soy sauce
1 tablespoon cornstarch

1. Fry chicken wings in as small amount of oil as possible until browned and tender; remove and drain on paper towels.
2. Meanwhile, heat vinegar, water, catsup, sugar, salt and soy sauce in saucepan.
3. Mix cornstarch with a small amount of water to make a paste; stir into sauce.
4. Cook and stir sweet-sour sauce until smooth, transparent and thickened.
5. Serve hot or cold as dipping sauce for chicken wings.

Teriyaki Chicken Wings

Makes 48 appetizers

24 chicken wings
1 cup naturally brewed soy sauce
¾ cup scallions with tops, chopped
⅓ cup sugar

4 teaspoons salad oil
1 clove garlic, crushed
1½ teaspoons ground ginger or
  1 tablespoon ginger root, grated

1. Disjoint chicken wings; discard tips.
2. Blend soy sauce, scallions, sugar, oil, garlic and ginger in large mixing bowl.
3. Stir in chicken pieces, cover, and marinate 30 minutes.
4. Remove chicken; reserve marinade.
5. Place chicken, side by side, in shallow baking pan, skin-side down; bake, uncovered, in preheated 350° F. oven 15 minutes.
6. Turn pieces over, baste with reserved marinade, and bake 15 minutes longer.

Chicken Tempura with Dipping Sauces

Serves 6

1 can (10¾ ounces) condensed
cream of shrimp soup
1 cup flour
1 egg, slightly beaten
salt
1 small eggplant (about ¾ pound),
peeled and cubed

3 chicken breasts, split, skinned and
boned (1½ pounds boneless)
1 medium Bermuda onion, sliced
1 medium green pepper, cut in
1-inch squares
corn or peanut oil
Sherry Soy Sauce
Mustard Sauce

1. In bowl, combine soup, flour, egg and ½ teaspoon salt; chill 30 minutes or until ready to use.
2. Meanwhile, salt eggplant; let stand 30 minutes. Pat dry.
3. Cut chicken into bite-size pieces.
4. Dip chicken and vegetables into soup batter to coat lightly.
5. Half-fill wok or large saucepan with oil; preheat to 375° F.
6. Cook chicken about 5 minutes, and vegetables about 3 minutes, a few pieces at a time, until golden.
7. Drain; keep warm. Serve with dipping sauces.

Sherry Soy Sauce

1½ cups

1 cup condensed beef broth
¼ cup soy sauce
¼ cup dry sherry

In small saucepan, combine ingredients; heat, stirring occasionally.

Mustard Sauce

Makes ½ cup

¼ cup dry mustard
¼ cup water

In small dish (about ½-cup size), combine mustard and water.

Crabmeat Won Tons

Makes 12 appetizers

⅓ cup cooked crabmeat, shredded
3 ounces cream cheese, softened
3 tablespoons water chestnuts,
  coarsely chopped
¼ teaspoon seasoned salt

12 won ton skins
1 egg, beaten
corn oil for deep frying
1 teaspoon original Worcestershire sauce

1. Combine crabmeat, cream cheese, water chestnuts, salt, and Worcestershire sauce.
2. Place won ton skin, point toward you, on counter; fill with ½ teaspoon crab mixture.
3. To seal, brush two edges with pastry brush dipped into beaten egg and close skin to make triangular shape.
4. Deep-fry in 375° F. oil until golden.

Fried Shrimp Toast

Makes 32 hors d'oeuvres

½ pound peeled and deveined
  raw shrimp, diced
6 water chestnuts, thinly chopped
1 egg, lightly beaten
1½ tablespoons cornstarch
1 teaspoon onion powder

¾ teaspoon salt
¼ teaspoon garlic powder
¼ teaspoon ground ginger
¼ teaspoon ground red pepper
8 slices firm, day-old white bread
2 tablespoons freeze-dried chives

1. Combine all ingredients except bread and chives; mix well to form a paste.
2. Trim crusts from bread; cut each slice into 4 triangles.
3. Spread triangles with shrimp mixture.
4. Preheat deep fat to 375° F.; add triangles, shrimp-side down, and fry 1 minute on each side.
5. Drain on paper towels.
6. Sprinkle with chives and serve immediately.

NOTE: If desired, fried shrimp toast may be wrapped in moisture-proof freezer paper or aluminum foil and frozen. Just before serving, reheat in a preheated 350° F. oven for 10 minutes.

Japanese Crab Tidbits

Makes 28 one-inch balls

1 tablespoon margarine
¼ cup cornstarch
¼ teaspoon salt
½ cup milk
2 tablespoons fine dry bread crumbs

1 can (6½ to 7½ ounces) crabmeat,
  drained and flaked
1 quart corn oil
soy sauce
prepared mustard

1. In small saucepan, melt margarine over low heat; stir in 1½ teaspoons cornstarch and salt until smooth.
2. Remove from heat; gradually stir in milk until smooth.
3. Bring to a boil over medium heat, stirring constantly; boil 1 minute.
4. Remove from heat; stir in bread crumbs and crabmeat.
5. Cover and refrigerate.
6. Shape into 1-inch balls; roll in remaining cornstarch, coating evenly.
7. Pour corn oil into heavy 3-quart saucepan or deep fryer, filling no more than ⅓ full; heat over medium heat to 375° F.
8. Carefully add crabmeat balls, a few at a time; fry 1 to 2 minutes, or until golden brown.
9. Drain on paper towels; serve with soy sauce and mustard.

Shrimp with Sweet & Sour Sauce

Makes 24 appetizers and 2 cups sauce

2 pounds (21 to 25 count per pound)
  raw, unpeeled shrimp
1 cup water
⅔ cup cider vinegar

⅔ cup brown sugar, packed
2 tablespoons cornstarch
2 tablespoons naturally brewed
  soy sauce

½ teaspoon Tabasco sauce

1. Peel shrimp, leaving tails on; devein.
2. Cook in boiling salted water 5 minutes; drain, cool, wrap, and refrigerate.
3. Combine 1 cup water, vinegar, brown sugar, cornstarch and soy sauce in saucepan; simmer, stirring constantly, until thickened, about 1 minute.
4. Cool, cover, and store at room temperature.
5. Arrange shrimp in serving bowl.
6. Add Tabasco to sweet-sour sauce; bring to a boil, stirring constantly.
7. Pour sauce into serving bowl over candle warmer and serve with shrimp.

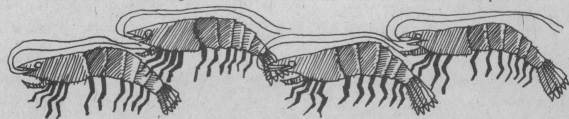

Seafood or Chicken Tempura
with Tempura Sauce

Serves 4

1 quart corn oil
1 pound fish: halibut, haddock or cod, cut in 1-inch strips, or 1 pound boned chicken, cut in 1-inch strips, or 1½ pounds medium-size shrimp, shelled and deveined
flour

vegetables: eggplant, squash, sweet potatoes, celery, green pepper, green beans, broccoli, carrots, cauliflower, mushrooms, or onions, cut in slices or in rings
Tempura Batter
cooked rice

Tempura Sauce or soy sauce

1. Pour corn oil into heavy, sturdy, flat-bottomed 3-quart saucepan or deep fryer, filling it no more than ⅓ full; heat over medium heat to 375° F.
2. Dust fish, chicken or shrimp lightly with flour. Dip them and vegetables in Tempura Batter.
3. Carefully add selected foods in single layer to prepared oil; fry, turning as needed, until tender, 1 to 2 minutes.
4. Drain on absorbent paper. Serve over rice with Tempura Sauce or soy sauce for dipping.

Tempura Batter

Makes enough batter to coat about 2 pounds fish or chicken or vegetables

¾ cup flour, sifted
¼ cup cornstarch
½ teaspoon baking powder

¼ teaspoon baking soda
1 cup water
1 egg

1. Sift together flour, cornstarch, baking powder and baking soda.
2. Stir in water, then egg; beat with rotary beater or wire whip until smooth and frothy.

Tempura Sauce

Makes about ¾ cup

½ cup apple juice or white wine
1 tablespoon soy sauce
¼ cup white radish, grated

1 teaspoon dry mustard
⅛ teaspoon ground ginger

Stir together apple juice or wine, soy sauce, radish, mustard and ginger until mixed.

Cantonese Meatballs with Orange Teriyaki Dip

Makes 4 dozen meatballs

1½ pounds ground beef
½ cup fine dry bread crumbs
1 teaspoon seasoned salt
¼ teaspoon seasoned pepper

1 egg, beaten
½ cup milk
2 tablespoons butter
Orange Teriyaki Dip

1. Combine all ingredients except butter; mix well.
2. Shape into tiny balls about ½-inch in diameter.
3. Melt butter; sauté meatballs until browned on all sides.
4. Keep warm and serve with Orange Teriyaki Dip.

Orange Teriyaki Dip

⅓ cup orange marmalade
1 clove garlic, peeled and minced
¼ cup teriyaki barbecue
   marinade

2 tablespoons fresh lemon juice
⅓ cup water
1 tablespoon cornstarch
2 tablespoons cold water

1. Combine marmalade, garlic, barbecue marinade, lemon juice and water; bring to a boil.
2. Reduce heat.
3. Combine cornstarch and cold water; add to teriyaki mixture.
4. Cook, stirring constantly, until mixture thickens. Serve with Cantonese Meatballs.

Rumaki

Makes about 15 appetizers

½ pound sliced bacon
½ pound chicken livers, halved
1 can (5 ounces) water chestnuts,
   drained and halved
4 scallions, cut into 1-inch lengths

⅓ cup imported soy sauce
½ teaspoon ground ginger
½ teaspoon ground turmeric
¼ teaspoon garlic powder
¼ teaspoon curry powder

1. Cut each strip of bacon in half, crosswise.
2. Wrap each half around 1 piece of liver, 1 chestnut half and 1 length of scallion; fasten with a toothpick.
3. Repeat with remaining bacon, liver, chestnuts and scallions; place in a small shallow pan.
4. Combine soy sauce, ginger, turmeric and garlic and curry powders; pour over contents in pan.
5. Cover and refrigerate for 2 hours.
6. Arrange on rack in broiler pan; place under a preheated hot broiler for 7 to 10 minutes, turning occasionally. Serve hot.

Chinese Pineapple Meatballs

Serves 10

For the Meatballs

2 pounds lean ground beef
½ cup celery, minced
½ cup almonds or pecans, chopped
2 teaspoons salt

½ cup cornflakes
4 eggs
2 tablespoons soy sauce
dash garlic powder
flour

vegetable oil for frying

1. Combine beef, celery, almonds, salt, cornflakes, eggs, soy sauce and garlic powder; form into small cocktail-size balls.
2. Roll in flour and fry in very hot oil; drain.
3. Pour sauce over meatballs and heat slowly.
4. When bubbly, pour into serving dish with warmer. Serve with toothpicks.

For the Sauce

2 cups chicken bouillon
1 cup sugar
6 tablespoons cornstarch
1 cup pineapple juice

¼-½ cup vinegar
2 tablespoons soy sauce
1 cup canned crushed pineapple, well drained

1 green pepper, chopped

1. Combine all ingredients except pineapple and green pepper; cook until thickened, stirring constantly.
2. Add crushed pineapple and green pepper.

Marinated Mushrooms

Makes about 3 dozen appetizers

1 pound small fresh mushrooms (about 36)
¼ cup onions, finely minced
¼ cup wine or rice wine vinegar

3 tablespoons dry sherry or sake
2 tablespoons imported soy sauce
2 tablespoons sugar
1 teaspoon salt

¼ teaspoon freshly ground black pepper

1. Trim stem ends from mushrooms; set aside.
2. In small saucepan, combine onions, wine, sherry, soy sauce, sugar, salt and pepper; bring to a boil.
3. Add mushrooms, stirring well. Let cool, stirring occasionally.
4. Cover and refrigerate about 24 hours.

Indonesian Beef Sate

Serves 4

1 medium onion, finely chopped
1 clove garlic, minced
½ cup dry vermouth or white wine
¼ cup corn syrup
¼ cup soy sauce
1 teaspoon ground coriander

1 teaspoon ground cumin seed
1 teaspoon ground ginger
1 teaspoon ground turmeric
1 pound boneless beef, cut into
   ½-inch cubes
Sate Sauce

1. In medium bowl, stir together onion, garlic, vermouth, corn syrup, soy sauce, coriander, cumin seed, ginger and turmeric; mix in beef.
2. Cover and refrigerate at least 3 hours.
3. Remove meat and thread on metal skewers.
4. Strain marinade to use as basting sauce, reserving onions for Sate Sauce.
5. Grill or broil 6 inches from source of heat, brushing often with strained marinade and turning frequently, 10 to 15 minutes, or until meat reaches desired doneness.
6. Serve with hot Sate Sauce.

Sate Sauce

Makes ¾ cup

1 tablespoon corn oil
reserved marinated onion (from
   Indonesian Sate)

¼ cup dry vermouth or white wine
¼ cup dark corn syrup
1 tablespoon soy sauce

1. Heat corn oil in small skillet over medium heat; add reserved marinated onion.
2. Cook, stirring constantly, 5 minutes, or until onions are soft.
3. Add vermouth, corn syrup and soy sauce; bring to a boil, stirring constantly.
4. Reduce heat and simmer 5 minutes.

Marinated Steak Appetizers

Makes 24 appetizers

1½ pounds top-grade lean beef
   sirloin
¼ cup sherry
2 tablespoons honey
⅓ cup soy sauce

2 tablespoons oyster sauce, available in Chinese markets and
   gourmet food stores
1 teaspoon fresh ginger, grated
pimiento-stuffed green olives

1. Cut beef into ½-inch cubes; set aside.
2. Combine sherry, honey, soy sauce, oyster sauce and ginger; pour over beef.
3. Marinate several hours for delicate flavor, overnight for more pronounced flavor.
4. Thread beef and green olives on skewers; broil to desired degree of doneness, turning as necessary. Serve piping hot.

Pork Satay Singapore

Serves 3 to 4

1 pound loin of pork, cut in bite-size pieces	1 onion, chopped
3 walnuts, ground	juice of 1 lemon (or lime)
½ teaspoon ginger root, minced	2 tablespoons soy sauce
2 cloves garlic, crushed	pinch sugar
	salt to taste

ground black pepper to taste

1. Combine all ingredients; let stand 1 hour (longer, if desired).
2. Thread pork on skewers; grill.

Egg Rolls
(Chinese Crêpes)

Makes 30 egg rolls

Pancake Wrappers

8 eggs	2 cups water
1½ cups all-purpose flour	shortening
1½ teaspoons salt	Pork Filling
½ teaspoon salad oil	

1. Beat eggs until light; add flour and salt, beating until smooth.
2. Add salad oil; stir in water.
3. Heat shortening in 6-inch skillet; spoon about 2 tablespoons batter into skillet; tilt until batter covers entire bottom skillet.
4. Fry over low heat until edges begin to curl away from skillet. Fry on one side only, then lift from pan and place on tray until all batter, with exception of ¼ cup is used.
5. Place a heaping tablespoon of filling on *fried* side of pancake.
6. Fold in 2 ends of pancake; brush edges with remaining batter to seal. Roll up other 2 edges to form into small roll.
7. Heat shortening to 360° F.; fry egg rolls until golden.

Pork Filling

½ pound cooked pork	½ pound cooked shrimp
1 large onion, peeled	1 can bean sprouts (#2 size)
½ pound or 1 can (6 ounces) mushrooms	½ teaspoon sesame oil
	2 teaspoons sesame seeds

1. Grind pork, onion and mushrooms through food chopper or food processor.
2. Mince shrimp; drain and chop bean sprouts.
3. Heat oil in saucepan; pour in sesame seeds and toast seeds.
4. Mix all ingredients in saucepan; cook until toasted.

Orange-Teriyaki Ribs, Microwaved

Serves 4

½ cup corn or peanut oil
½ cup soy sauce
½ cup fresh orange juice
1 teaspoon orange rind, grated
4 scallions, chopped

2 tablespoons brown sugar
1 green pepper, chopped
1 clove garlic, minced
2 teaspoons ground ginger
2 pounds spareribs, cut into 4 pieces

1. Mix together all ingredients except ribs in 12 x 8-inch glass baking dish.
2. Add ribs; turn to coat both sides.
3. Marinate in refrigerator, covered, overnight, turning frequently.
4. Remove ribs from marinade, reserving marinade; arrange ribs in clean 12 x 8-inch glass baking dish with small ends of bone toward center of dish.
5. **To Dry Roast:** Cover ribs with waxed paper. Microcook on HIGH 5 minutes. Microcook on 50 percent power, rotating ribs and dish every 10 minutes, for 30 to 35 minutes, or until fork-tender. Baste with the marinade; microcook, uncovered, on HIGH 5 minutes. Let stand 5 minutes. **OR To Braise:** Add 1 cup water to baking dish. Cover tightly with plastic wrap; pierce wrap with fork. Microcook on HIGH 5 minutes. Microcook on 50 percent power, rotating ribs and dish every 10 minutes, for 35 to 40 minutes, or until fork-tender. Drain off liquids. Baste with marinade; microcook, uncovered, on HIGH 5 minutes. Let stand 5 minutes.

Samosas

Makes about 48

peanut oil
½ cup onion, finely chopped
2 teaspoons ginger, finely chopped
1 teaspoon fennel seed
¾ teaspoon salt
½ teaspoon mustard

¼ teaspoon ground cumin seed
¼ teaspoon turmeric
½ cup water
2 cups cooked potatoes, finely diced
2 packages (10 ounces each) pastry mix

1. Heat ¼ cup peanut oil in large skillet; add onion and ginger and sauté until onion is tender, about 5 minutes.
2. Stir in fennel, salt, mustard, cumin, turmeric, water and potatoes; reduce heat to low, cover skillet tightly, and cook for 5 minutes.
3. Transfer potato mixture to bowl; cool to room temperature.
4. Meanwhile, prepare pastry dough according to package directions.
5. On lightly floured board, roll out the dough into two 15-inch squares; cut into 3-inch squares.
6. Place a slightly rounded teaspoon of potato mixture in center of each square.
7. Moisten edges with water; bring opposite corners together to form a triangle. Pinch seam together well, then press edge with tines of fork.
8. Fry several samosas at a time in deep hot (375° F.) peanut oil until golden on each side, about 2 minutes.
9. Drain on paper towels; serve warm.

Char Siu

Makes 48 appetizers

2 pounds boneless pork roast
½ cup naturally brewed soy sauce
⅓ cup honey
¼ cup sherry

1 teaspoon red food coloring
¼ teaspoon garlic powder
¼ teaspoon ground ginger
Mustard Soy Sauce

toasted sesame seed

1. Cut pork roast lengthwise into 3 strips; place in large shallow pan.
2. Combine soy sauce, honey, sherry, food coloring, garlic powder and ginger; pour over pork, turning several times to coat thoroughly.
3. Cover and marinate in refrigerator 24 hours, turning occasionally.
4. Remove pork from marinade and lay on rack placed over pan of water; insert meat thermometer into thickest part of one strip.
5. Roast in preheated 325° F. oven 30 minutes. Turn strips over and roast 20 minutes longer, or until meat thermometer registers 170° F.
6. Remove pork from rack; cool at room temperature.
7. At serving time, cut strips into thin slices; dip each slice of Char Siu into Mustard Soy Sauce, then into toasted sesame seed.

NOTE: Sesame seeds can be "toasted" by frying in few drops of vegetable oil on top of stove (or baked slowly in 200° F. oven until brown).

Mustard Soy Sauce

2 tablespoons dry mustard
water

naturally brewed soy sauce
toasted sesame seed

Blend dry mustard with enough water to make a smooth paste; cover and let stand 5 minutes. Thin with soy sauce to dipping consistency.

Fried Rice Rolls

Serves 6

½ cup scallions, sliced
2 tablespoons vegetable oil
2 cups cooked rice
1 can (8 ounces) water chestnuts, sliced
1 cup cooked chicken, diced

1 cup cooked shrimp, diced
3 tablespoons soy sauce
⅛ teaspoon ground black pepper
2 eggs, slightly beaten
ripe olives (optional garnish)
radish roses (optional garnish)

12 lettuce leaves

1. Sauté scallions in oil until tender-crisp. Stir in rice, water chestnuts, chicken, shrimp, soy sauce, and pepper; cook until thoroughly heated.
2. Stir in eggs; continue cooking, stirring constantly, until eggs are done.
3. Spoon mixture onto serving dish; garnish with ripe olives or radish roses, if desired.
4. Arrange lettuce leaves on separate plate. Spoon fried rice onto lettuce leaves; roll up neatly. Eat with fingers while hot.

Bombay Curried Banana Chicken Chowder

Serves 5 to 6

¼ cup butter (or margarine)
1 medium onion, chopped
1 stalk celery, chopped
2 tablespoons flour
2 cups chicken broth

1 cup light cream
1 teaspoon curry powder
½ teaspoon salt
1½ cups cooked chicken, diced
2 bananas, peeled and diced

1. Melt butter in large saucepan; stir in onion and celery. Cook until vegetables are limp.
2. Stir in flour; mix well.
3. Stir in chicken broth, cream, curry powder and salt; simmer several minutes.
4. Add chicken and bananas; heat to boiling.
5. Serve hot.

NOTE: Hearty enough to make a good main dish offering followed by a crisp salad!

Japanese Chicken Soup with Noodles

Serves 4 to 6

6 cups fat-free chicken stock
2 teaspoons soy sauce
salt to taste (optional)
2 ounces cooked udon* noodles or
  narrow egg noodles

6 large Oriental mushrooms,
  soaked in warm water until
  softened, then sliced
½ cup cooked chicken, diced
4 to 6 pieces lemon peel

1. Heat together chicken stock, soy sauce and salt, if needed.
2. Add noodles, mushrooms and chicken; bring to a boil.
3. Serve piping hot with lemon peel.

*NOTE: Udon, a very soft large white noodle, available in some supermarkets or Oriental grocers, must be pre-cooked before adding to soup. Otherwise, soup will become cloudy.

Chinese Rice Soup

Serves 8 to 10

3 cans (10¾ ounces each) condensed
  chicken broth
3 soup cans water
2 cups cooked chicken, cubed
1 package (10 ounces) frozen
  chopped spinach

1 cup celery, thinly sliced
¼ cup soy sauce
½ teaspoon ground ginger
1 cup quick-cooking rice,
  uncooked
½ cup radishes, sliced

1. Combine all ingredients except rice and radishes in large saucepan; bring to a boil.
2. Add rice and radishes; reduce heat and simmer 5 minutes, or until done, stirring occasionally.
3. Serve with additional soy, if desired.

Cantonese Sweet & Sour Soup

Serves 4

4 cups chicken broth
½ cooked chicken breast, cut
  in julienne strips
½ small can bamboo shoots, diced
½ small can mushrooms, sliced

1 tablespoon fresh lemon juice
salt to taste
¼ teaspoon ground pepper
1 tablespoon soy sauce
1 large egg, beaten

1. Heat chicken broth. Add chicken, bamboo shoots and mushrooms; simmer 5 minutes.
2. Add lemon juice, salt to taste, pepper and soy sauce; heat through, stirring continually.
3. Add egg; stir one minute longer, but do not boil.
4. Taste to correct seasonings and serve.

NOTE: *Great for the dieter, especially if consumed with broiled fish or kabobs. Fresh spinach or chopped celery make fine additions!*

Egg Drop Soup

Serves 8

3 quarts water
9 chicken bouillon cubes
⅓ cup naturally brewed soy sauce

6 eggs, well beaten
1½ cups scallions and tops,
  finely chopped

1. Bring water to a boil in large saucepan; add bouillon cubes and stir until dissolved.
2. Stir in soy sauce; bring to a boil again.
3. Remove from heat; add eggs all at once, stirring rapidly in a circle with a spoon. (Eggs will separate to form fine threads.)
4. Stir in scallions; serve immediately.

Lotus Soup

Serves 4 to 5

1 cup celery, diagonally sliced
½ cup scallions, diagonally sliced
⅛ teaspoon ground ginger
3 tablespoons butter or margarine
1 can (10¾ ounces) condensed
  cream of chicken soup

1 can (10¾ ounces) condensed
  chicken broth
1½ soup cans water
1 cup cabbage or Chinese cabbage,
  cut in long thin shreds
1 cup fresh spinach, chopped

1 teaspoon soy sauce

1. Cook celery and scallions with ginger in butter in saucepan until tender.
2. Stir in soups and water.
3. Add remaining ingredients; heat, stirring occasionally.

Sweet & Sour Chicken Soup Salmagundi

Serves 8 to 10

1 (3-pound) chicken, cut up
water
4 peppercorns
1 tablespoon celery seeds
1 teaspoon whole cloves
2 tablespoons ginger root, sliced
1 tablespoon sesame oil
½ teaspoon garlic powder
¼ cup white vinegar
½ cup brown sugar, packed
¼ cup catsup
1 tablespoon soy sauce
1 teaspoon original Worcestershire sauce
¼ cup cornstarch
1 can (14½ ounces) whole tomatoes,
  diced

1 cup onion, cut in ½-inch cubes
¾ cup green pepper, cut in ½-inch
  cubes
1 cup celery, sliced
1 daikon radish, sliced
1½ cups Chinese winter melon, cubed
  (optional)
1 package (10 ounces) frozen
  Italian green beans
1 can (8 ounces) pineapple tidbits,
  drained
¼ teaspoon red pepper
salt
2 cans (3½ ounces each) water
  chestnuts, drained and sliced
sesame seeds (for garnish)

1. Place chicken in enough water to cover.
2. Tie together in cheesecloth bag peppercorns, celery seeds, cloves and ginger root; add to water and simmer 1 hour.
3. Remove chicken, cool, then pull meat from bones; dice meat and set aside.
4. Skim and discard fat from chicken stock.
5. Add to remaining stock sesame oil, garlic powder, vinegar, sugar, catsup, soy sauce and Worcestershire; bring to a boil.
6. Meanwhile, add ½ cup water to cornstarch, mixing to make a thin paste; add paste to chicken stock, stirring rapidly to avoid lumping.
7. Add tomatoes, onion, green pepper, celery, radish, winter melon, green beans and pineapple; cook 15 minutes.
8. Add red pepper and season to taste with salt; cook 5 minutes.
9. Return diced chicken to pot, add sliced water chestnuts, and heat through.
10. Ladle into bowls and garnish with sesame seeds.

NOTE: This soup is hearty and filling, hence its name Salmagundi!

Oyster Stew Orientale

Serves 3 to 4

½ cup chopped onion
2 tablespoons butter or margarine
1 can (10½ ounces) condensed
  oyster stew

1 soup can milk
1 tablespoon toasted sesame seeds
cooked rice
chopped chives (for garnish)

1. Cook onion in butter in saucepan until tender.
2. Add soup, milk, and sesame seeds; heat, stirring occasionally.
3. Spoon about ¼ cup rice in each bowl, pour in soup, and garnish with chives.

Korean Wedding Beef Soup
with Meatballs

Serves 6

1½ pounds stewing beef
1½ quarts water or beef broth,
  diluted
4 cloves garlic
4 scallions, chopped
1 large Bermuda onion, peeled
  and sliced
3 tablespoons corn oil

6 large ripe tomatoes or 1 can
  (20 ounces) canned tomatoes
2 teaspoons pine nuts
freshly ground black pepper to taste
4 ounces Chinese vermicelli
  (thin noodles)
2 to 3 tablespoons soy sauce
Meatballs

parsley

1. Put beef into stockpot with water; cover and cook slowly.
2. Meanwhile, sauté garlic, scallions and onion in oil until vegetables soften.
3. Add tomatoes, pine nuts and pepper; cook until tomatoes soften.
4. Add mixture to stockpot; cover and simmer 1½ hours, or until meat is tender.
5. Remove meat; reserve for other dishes.
6. Add vermicelli to soup; cook until tender.
7. Add soy sauce and Meatballs; cook until Meatballs are heated through.
8. Serve soup in tureen sprinkled with egg shreds and parsley.

Meatballs

1 pound ground beef, pork,
  chicken or duck
2 tablespoons onion, minced
1/16 teaspoon freshly ground black pepper
½ teaspoon fresh ginger, grated
½ teaspoon salt

1 tablespoon ground sesame seed
1 tablespoon flour
1 egg, beaten
3 tablespoons peanut or corn oil
1 egg white
1 teaspoon water

1. Mix together beef, onion, pepper, ginger, ¼ teaspoon salt and sesame seed; form into 1½-inch balls.
2. Roll balls in flour, then in egg.
3. Heat peanut oil in small skillet; brown balls on all sides slowly in hot oil.
4. Drain meatballs on absorbent paper; set aside.
5. Combine egg white, water and remaining ¼ teaspoon salt; fry quickly in same skillet in which meatballs were fried.
6. Remove from skillet when egg has just set; roll up, cut into shreds with sharp knife, and set aside.
7. Add meatballs to soup to heat through.

NOTE: This is a famous dish served at festive occasions including weddings!

Bombay Chicken Salad

Serves 6 to 8

4 cups cooked chicken, cut in
  large chunks
1 cup celery, cut in diagonal slices
1 cup California dried figs, chopped
½ cup cashew nuts, chopped
½ cup evaporated milk

⅔ cup mayonnaise
1 teaspoon salt
⅛ teaspoon pepper
½ teaspoon curry powder
1 tablespoon vinegar
crisp salad greens

1. Combine chicken with celery, figs and nuts in mixing bowl.
2. Blend milk with mayonnaise, salt, pepper, curry and vinegar in small bowl; add to chicken and toss lightly.
3. Serve on crisp greens.

NOTE: *Fresh or dried figs are a real favorite with Asians.*

Chinese Almond Rice Salad with Soy Dressing

Serves 4 to 6

⅓ cup whole natural almonds
1 teaspoon soy sauce
Soy Dressing
3 cups cooked long-grain rice

1½ cups cooked chicken, shredded
1 cup celery, diagonally sliced
½ cup scallions, sliced
1 small head Chinese cabbage

preserved kumquats (optional garnish)

1. Place almonds in shallow baking pan and toss with soy sauce; spread in single layer.
2. Toast in preheated 300° F. oven 15 minutes, stirring frequently; set aside to cool.
3. Prepare Soy Dressing; set aside.
4. Combine rice, chicken, celery and scallions.
5. Reserve outer green cabbage leaves to line serving bowl; shred enough remaining cabbage to measure 2 cups and add to rice mixture.
6. Add ⅔ cup Soy Dressing and toasted almonds; toss.
7. Line serving bowl with reserved cabbage leaves; spoon salad into bowl. Garnish with kumquats, if desired.
8. Serve at once, passing remaining Soy Dressing.

Soy Dressing

Makes about 1 cup

½ cup corn oil
3 tablespoons soy sauce
2 tablespoons vinegar
2 tablespoons catsup

2 teaspoons brown sugar
¼ teaspoon garlic powder
¼ teaspoon ground ginger or
  grated fresh ginger root

Combine oil, soy sauce, vinegar, catsup, brown sugar, garlic powder and ginger in a jar; cover tightly and shake well to blend.

Chinese Chicken Salad Le Grand Buffet with Dijon Sherry Dressing

Serves 8

4 whole chicken breasts
1½ cups chicken broth
1 bunch scallions, sliced diagonally
ice water
1 cup water chestnuts, sliced

1 cup sesame seeds, toasted lightly
1 pound Chinese pea pods, trimmed
  and cut in julienne strips
Dijon Sherry Dressing
salt to taste
pepper to taste

1. Poach chicken breasts in chicken broth over medium heat 20 minutes, or until done. Let cool in broth.
2. Lift chicken from broth; remove skin and cut meat into ¼-inch slices.
3. Crisp scallions in ice water in bowl; drain.
4. Mix chicken, water chestnuts, sesame seeds, pea pods and scallions in large bowl; toss with as much Dijon Sherry Dressing as desired.
5. Season to taste with salt and pepper.

Dijon Sherry Dressing

1 ginger root, peeled and cubed
¼ cup dry sherry
2 egg yolks
2 tablespoons Dijon prepared mustard
2 teaspoons sugar

juice of 1 lemon
½ cup corn or peanut oil
½ cup sesame oil
2 tablespoons soy sauce
salt to taste
pepper to taste

1. Marinate ginger root in sherry several hours, or overnight.
2. Beat egg yolks with mustard; add sugar and lemon juice, stirring to dissolve.
3. Combine oils; add oils in thin stream to yolk mixture, whisking constantly until thickened and smooth.
4. Remove ginger root from sherry; add sherry to yolk mixture with soy sauce.
5. Season to taste with salt and pepper.

Chang's Cucumber Salad

Serves 3 to 4

2 large cucumbers
1 teaspoon sea salt
scant 2 tablespoons soy sauce

pinch natural sugar (available in
  health food stores)
1 teaspoon sesame oil

1. Wash and peel cucumbers; slice into thin rounds. Sprinkle with sea salt; let stand several hours. Rinse under cold water; dry on paper towels.
2. Blend together soy sauce and sugar; pour over cucumbers in shallow dish.
3. Cover and refrigerate several hours.
4. Add sesame oil; serve very cold.

Far-East Spinach Salad

Serves 6

2 pounds spinach (or beet tops),
  steamed
¼ cup peanut (or safflower) oil

juice of 1 lemon
small red onion, minced
handful sesame seeds

dash of salt

Mix all ingredients together; serve cold.

Teriyaki Salad

Serves 4

1 large head iceberg lettuce
Teriyaki Salad Dressing
4 half-breasts of chicken
4 squares (1-inch) green pepper

8 diagonal slices zucchini,
  cut 1 inch thick
8 cherry tomatoes
4 mushrooms, halved

1. Core, rinse, and thoroughly drain lettuce; chill well.
2. Prepare Teriyaki Salad Dressing; set aside.
3. Remove skin and bones from chicken; cut each breast into thirds lengthwise.
4. Thread three strips chicken, ripple-fashion, onto each of 4 bamboo skewers.
5. Parboil green pepper and zucchini 1 minute; drain.
6. Thread vegetables onto 4 other skewers, along with tomatoes and mushrooms.
7. Broil chicken skewers 5 inches from heat 10 minutes, basting well with Teriyaki Salad Dressing, turning often.
8. Add vegetable skewers for the last 5 minutes chicken cooks, turning and basting with dressing often.
9. Cut lettuce into bite-size chunks to measure 2 quarts.
10. Arrange 1 chicken and 1 vegetable skewer on a bed of lettuce for each serving; pass remaining dressing.

Teriyaki Salad Dressing

Makes 1 cup

½ cup beef consommé
¼ cup corn oil
2 tablespoons naturally brewed
  soy sauce

2 tablespoons dry sherry
2 tablespoons white wine vinegar
1 small clove garlic, peeled and
  minced

¼ teaspoon ground ginger

1. Combine consommé, oil, soy sauce, sherry, vinegar, garlic and ginger in small jar.
2. Cover jar and shake well to blend; shake again just before serving.

NOTE: Total salad: 1475 calories; Per serving: 369 calories.

Jade Tree Iceberg Salad

Serves 6

1 head western iceberg lettuce
¼ cup sesame seeds
1⅓ cups salad oil
⅔ cup tarragon vinegar
2 teaspoons salt
1 teaspoon dry mustard
few drops garlic, crushed

½ teaspoon freshly ground pepper
¼ cup sugar
½ cup celery, finely minced
1 can (5 ounces) water chestnuts, drained, rinsed and sliced
2 cups cooked chicken, cut in julienne strips

1. Core, rinse, and thoroughly drain lettuce; refrigerate in disposable plastic bag.
2. Toast sesame seeds in ungreased pan over low heat, stirring frequently, until lightly browned; cool.
3. Combine oil, vinegar, seasonings and sugar in 1-quart jar with tight-fitting lid; cover and shake until well blended.
4. Add sesame seeds and celery; shake again.
5. Tear lettuce into bowl; add dressing, tossing lightly to coat well.
6. Top with water chestnuts and chicken and serve.

Indonesian Vegetable Salad with Peanut Dressing

Serves 8

5 cups cabbage, coarsely chopped
boiling salted water
1 package (10 ounces) frozen French-style green beans
1½ cups cocktail peanuts
2 tablespoons firmly packed light brown sugar
1 teaspoon onion salt

½ teaspoon salt
2 tablespoons fresh lemon juice
1 can (1 pound) bean sprouts, drained
1 cucumber, peeled and sliced
½ cup sliced radishes
2 hard-cooked eggs (for garnish)
hot cherry peppers (for garnish)

1. Cook cabbage in boiling salted water until tender-crisp; drain and reserve water.
2. Cook green beans half as long as package directs after coming to a boil; drain and reserve water.
3. Chill cabbage and green beans.
4. Combine vegetable waters; set aside 1 cup.
5. In blender container, combine cocktail peanuts, light brown sugar, onion salt, salt, lemon juice and reserved 1 cup vegetable water; blend until fairly smooth, then chill.
6. To serve, layer cabbage, green beans, bean sprouts, cucumber and radishes on large platter; garnish platter with wedged or sliced hard-cooked eggs and hot peppers. Serve with prepared dressing.

Cantonese Walnut Lobster Salad
with Sweet & Sour Dressing

Serves 6

1 tablespoon butter
1 tablespoon soy sauce
1 cup California walnuts, large
   pieces and halves
1 cup diagonally sliced celery
1 can (5 ounces) water chestnuts,
   drained and sliced

½ cup sliced scallions
1 can (11 ounces) Mandarin orange
   sections, drained
3 cups cooked lobster chunks (or
   prawns, crab or tuna)
Sweet & Sour Dressing
watercress or salad greens

1. Melt butter; add soy sauce and walnuts, stirring gently over low heat until walnuts are lightly toasted, about 10 minutes.
2. Remove from heat and cool.
3. Combine well-chilled celery, water chestnuts, scallions, Mandarin orange sections and lobster.
4. Add just enough Sweet & Sour Dressing to hold ingredients together; fold in walnuts.
5. Pile on crisp watercress or salad greens; serve with additional dressing, if desired.

Sweet & Sour Dressing

Makes about 3 cups

3 eggs
½ cup sugar
2 tablespoons all-purpose flour
2 teaspoons seasoned salt

⅛ teaspoon curry powder
⅓ cup strained fresh lemon juice
⅓ cup cider vinegar
1 can (14½ ounces) evaporated milk

1 tablespoon soft (or melted) butter

1. Beat eggs.
2. Mix sugar, flour, salt and curry powder; beat into eggs.
3. Blend in lemon juice and vinegar.
4. Cook in top of double boiler over boiling water until mixture thickens, about 10 minutes, stirring frequently to keep smooth.
5. Beat in undiluted evaporated milk and butter.
6. Cool and store in covered container in refrigerator.

NOTE: A delicately flavored dressing to use on seafood and fruit salad particularly.

Marinated Celery & Shrimp Salad

Serves 4 to 6

1 bunch celery
1 cup salted water
⅓ cup soy sauce
2 tablespoons scallions, minced
2 tablespoons white vinegar
1 tablespoon dry white wine

1 teaspoon salad oil
½ teaspoon sugar
¼ teaspoon ground ginger
1 pound cooked, deveined shrimp, peeled

1. Trim ends of celery, reserving leaves for garnish; separate celery into ribs and cut into 2-inch lengths.
2. In a saucepan, bring salted water to a boil; add celery.
3. Reduce heat, cover, and simmer for 8 minutes, or until celery is crisp-tender.
4. Drain; place celery in bowl.
5. Combine soy sauce, scallions, vinegar, wine, oil, sugar and ginger; mix well.
6. Pour half the marinade over celery; cover and chill 1 hour. Pour other half marinade over shrimp; cover and chill for 1 hour.
7. Arrange drained, chilled celery at one side of platter and drained, chilled shrimp at the other side; garnish with celery leaves.

Asian Vegetable Salad with Ginger Soy Dressing

Serves 2

2 cups sliced mushrooms
1 cup celery, sliced
1 cup Chinese pea pods
1 can (8 ounces) water chestnuts, drained and sliced

Ginger Soy Dressing
1 cup cooked chicken, shredded
shredded iceberg lettuce
2 cherry tomatoes, halved (for garnish)

1. Arrange mushrooms, celery, pea pods and water chestnuts in 2-quart shallow casserole dish; pour Ginger Soy Dressing over vegetables.
2. Cover and refrigerate 2 hours.
3. Drain, reserving marinade.
4. Arrange vegetables and chicken on serving plate lined with shredded lettuce; garnish with cherry tomatoes.

Ginger Soy Dressing

1 clove garlic, pressed
½ cup corn oil
3 tablespoons soy sauce

2 tablespoons white wine vinegar
1 tablespoon ginger root, chopped
2 teaspoons prepared mustard
3 tablespoons fresh lemon or lime juice

Combine garlic, oil, soy sauce, vinegar, ginger, mustard and lemon or lime juice in screw-top jar; shake well.

Tuna Chinese Almond Salad

Serves 4

2 cans (7 ounces each) tuna in
    vegetable oil
2 cups lettuce, coarsely shredded
¼ cup scallions, chopped
½ cup parsley, chopped
¼ teaspoon lemon rind, grated

1 tablespoon fresh lemon juice
¼ cup corn oil
3 tablespoons soy sauce
½ teaspoon ground coriander
¼ cup sesame seeds
¼ cup toasted almonds, slivered

1 can (3 ounces) chow mein noodles

1. Place tuna chunks, lettuce, scallions and parsley in large bowl; chill.
2. Mix lemon rind, lemon juice, corn oil, soy sauce and coriander; pour over tuna mixture.
3. Sprinkle salad with sesame seeds, almonds and chow mein noodles; toss and serve immediately.

Gourmet Beef Salad

Serves 6

⅓ cup warm water
½ cup seedless raisins
2 cups cooked roast beef, cut in
    julienne strips
1½ cups fresh pineapple pieces
½ cup celery, chopped

½ small green pepper, cut in strips
¼ cup stuffed green olives, sliced
¼ cup slivered almonds
1 tablespoon pimiento, chopped
¼ teaspoon salt
½ cup dairy sour cream

flaked coconut (optional)

1. Add water to raisins; let stand 15 minutes, then drain.
2. Combine roast beef, raisins, pineapple, celery, green pepper, olives, almonds, pimiento and salt; toss lightly.
3. Add sour cream; mix until coated.
4. Chill mixture 2 to 3 hours in refrigerator.
5. Top with flaked coconut, if desired.

Honey Banana Salad

Serves 4

¼ cup peanut oil
¼ cup fresh lemon juice
2 tablespoons honey
½ teaspoon ground ginger
½ teaspoon sea salt
½ head lettuce, shredded

1 small green pepper, cut into
    julienne strips
2 bananas, sliced
¼ cup coconut (fresh, preferably),
    shredded

1. Combine oil, lemon juice, honey, ginger and salt in small jar with a tight-fitting lid; shake well to blend.
2. Pour over lettuce, green pepper, bananas and coconut in a medium-size bowl; toss to mix.

Dragon Whiskers Salad

Serves 3 to 4

1 pound bunch fresh asparagus	pinch sugar
boiling salted water	pinch salt
1 tablespoon wine vinegar	½ teaspoon ginger root, minced

¼ teaspoon sesame oil

1. Break off and discard tough ends of asparagus; scrub spears with stiff brush under running water to remove any sand.
2. Break each spear and tender parts into 2-inch pieces.
3. Barely cook (4 minutes) asparagus in boiling salted water; drain.
4. Rinse immediately under cold running water; drain.
5. Mix together vinegar, sugar, salt, ginger and sesame oil; marinate "whiskers" in vinegar-sesame dressing a few minutes before serving.

NOTE: *Make "whiskers" hot by using few drops Tabasco and ground Szechuan pepper to taste (use sparingly!). Also corn or peanut oil can be substituted for sesame oil.*

Korean Eggplant Salad

Serves 6

1 large or 2 small eggplants	½ clove garlic, crushed
boiling water	1 teaspoon sesame oil
2 tablespoons corn oil	few dashes Tabasco (or cayenne)
1½ tablespoons vinegar	to taste
pinch sugar	1 tablespoon toasted sesame seeds

1 teaspoon soy or oyster sauce

1. Cover eggplant with boiling water; cook until barely tender.
2. Drain, cool, and peel; cut into julienne strips ½ inch long.
3. Mix oil, vinegar, sugar, garlic, sesame oil, Tabasco (or cayenne), sesame seeds and soy (or oyster sauce); pour over eggplant.
4. Cover and refrigerate 1 or 2 hours; drain.
5. Serve with boiled or broiled fish or as part of lettuce lunch.

NOTE: *Sesame oil is availabe in Oriental or health food shops. Sesame seeds can be "toasted" by frying in few drops vegetable oil on top of stove (or baked slowly in 200° F. oven until brown).*

Almond Chicken, Chow Style
Serves 4

2 whole chicken breasts
1 cup orange juice
2 chicken bouillon cubes, crushed
2 tablespoons cornstarch
2 tablespoons catsup
2 tablespoons steak sauce
1 tablespoon vinegar
4 teaspoons sugar
1 teaspoon salt

1 cup scallions, sliced
½ cup radishes, sliced
1 can (4 or 5 ounces) water chestnuts, drained and sliced
1 can (8 ounces) green beans or 1 cup fresh green beans, cooked
2 tablespoons salad oil
½ cup slivered almonds
crisp chow mein noodles

1. Remove chicken meat from bones and discard skin; cut meat into ½ inch cubes.
2. Mix orange juice, bouillon cubes, cornstarch, catsup, steak sauce, vinegar, sugar and ½ teaspoon salt; set aside.
3. Prepare all vegetables. (There won't be time once cooking begins!)
4. Heat oil in skillet until a piece of chicken sizzles when added; add all chicken and sprinkle with ½ teaspoon salt.
5. Stir-fry over medium heat for 10 minutes, or until chicken is cooked and golden.
6. Add almonds to pan; stir-fry 1 minute.
7. Mix in scallions until coated with oil; add orange juice mixture and cook, stirring gently, until it comes to a boil and is thickened.
8. Add radishes, water chestnuts, and beans; cook just until heated through.
9. Serve as soon as possible over chow mein noodles.

Chicken Cashew
Serves 6 to 8

3 whole chicken breasts (6 halves)
½ pound Chinese pea pods, or 2 packages frozen
1 cup mushrooms, sliced
½ cup scallions, sliced
1 can (6 ounces) bamboo shoots, drained
½ cup water chestnuts, sliced

1 chicken bouillon cube
¼ cup soy sauce
1 to 2 tablespoons water
2 tablespoons cornstarch
½ teaspoon sugar
dash of pepper
½ teaspoon salt
4 ounces cashew nuts

hot cooked rice

1. Skin, bone and cut chicken into small bite-size pieces; set aside.
2. Break off ends and remove strings from pea pods; set aside.
3. Prepare mushrooms, scallions, bamboo shoots and water chestnuts; set aside.
4. Mix together chicken bouillon, soy sauce, water, cornstarch, sugar, pepper and salt; set aside.
5. Put chicken in a stovetop casserole; cook, covered, until opaque and tender, about 15 minutes, stirring several times while cooking.
6. Stir in pea pods, mushrooms and scallions; cook, covered, 2 minutes.
7. Add bamboo shoots, water chestnuts, and reserved soy sauce mixture; stir and cook, covered, until sauce is thickened and food is well-heated throughout, about 3 minutes. Stir in cashew nuts. Serve with rice.

Angostura Oriental Chicken

Serves 4

2 tablespoons butter or margarine
1 pound skinless and boneless chicken
  breasts, cut into strips
1 cup celery, sliced
1 bunch scallions, trimmed and sliced
1 can (6 ounces) sliced mushrooms,
  drained
1 can (8 ounces) water chestnuts,
  drained and cut into slices

1 jar (4 ounces) pimientos, drained
  and diced
1 can (10¾ ounces) condensed
  golden mushroom soup
1 tablespoon Angostura aromatic
  bitters
2 tablespoons soy sauce
hot cooked rice
crisp noodles (optional)

1. Heat butter in large skillet; brown chicken.
2. Add remaining ingredients; simmer for 15 minutes, stirring occasionally.
3. Serve spooned over rice, topped with crisp noodles, if desired.

Chinese Smoked Chicken in Bag

Serves 4 to 6

1 (4-pound) roasting chicken
1½ tablespoons salt
boiling water

5 tablespoons light or dark
  brown sugar
1 tablespoon soy sauce
1 tablespoon sesame oil

1. Wash chicken and pat-dry with paper towels; rub inside and out with salt.
2. Refrigerate, loosely covered with waxed paper, for at least 6 hours, or overnight.
3. Pour enough boiling water into steamer or large roasting kettle with cooking rack to come within 1 inch of rack.
4. Set large heat-proof plate (at least ½ inch smaller in diameter than steamer) 2 inches above water on 2 small heat-proof dishes or bowls. Bring water to boil.
5. Place chicken on large plate and cover pot securely; steam chicken 40 minutes, adding more water if needed.
6. Line bottom of deep, heavy, large flameproof casserole with foil; sprinkle foil with brown sugar.
7. Place chicken on wire rack; set rack over sugared foil.
8. Line inside of casserole lid with foil, bring it up over edges to ensure that it fits casserole tightly and to prevent any smoke from escaping.
9. Cover casserole and place on stove over medium heat 10 minutes; turn off heat and let chicken rest 5 minutes.
10. Lift out smoked chicken onto board or plate.
11. Mix soy sauce and sesame oil; brush on chicken.
12. Place chicken in brown paper bag; secure bag so no heat can escape.
13. Place bag on small sheet pan and bake in preheated 350° F. oven 15 minutes.
14. Remove chicken from oven; let stand at least 10 minutes.
15. Carve chicken; serve hot or cold with pan drippings, if desired.

Banana & Chicken Stir-Fry

Serves 6 to 8

4 whole chicken breasts, cut in
  half, boned and skinned
2 tablespoons butter or margarine
3 cups broccoli flowerets
¼ cup onion, chopped

1 tablespoon soy sauce
1 teaspoon salt
½ teaspoon dried basil
⅛ teaspoon pepper
2 tomatoes, cut in wedges

4 bananas

1. Cut each breast half into 10 to 12 thin strips.
2. Melt butter in large skillet; add chicken, broccoli and onion; cook until chicken is white and onion is tender.
3. Add soy sauce, salt, basil, pepper and tomatoes; cover and cook over medium heat for 5 minutes.
4. Peel bananas, cut into 1-inch diagonal slices, and add to skillet; cover and cook about 1 minute (just until bananas are heated).

Sweet 'n' Sour Chicken

Serves 4 to 6

3 whole chicken breasts, boned
  and skinned
2 tablespoons cornstarch
⅓ cup peanut oil
2 cloves garlic, crushed
½ large green pepper, seeded
  and cut into thin strips

1 can (8½ ounces) pineapple
  tidbits, undrained
½ cup sweet mixed pickles, coarsely
  chopped
¼ cup sweet mixed pickle juice
3 tablespoons soy sauce
1 medium tomato cut in wedges

hot cooked rice

1. Cut chicken into narrow strips; dredge with 1 tablespoon cornstarch.
2. Heat peanut oil in large skillet; add chicken and garlic. Sauté, stirring, over medium-high heat until chicken is white and tender.
3. Mix in green pepper, pineapple (with syrup), pickles and pickle juice; bring mixture to a boil.
4. Blend together soy sauce and remaining cornstarch; stir into boiling mixture.
5. Add tomato wedges; cook 1 minute longer.
6. Serve immediately with rice.

Chinese Chicken with Peanuts

Serves 4

2 pounds chicken breasts, boned
and skinned
¼ cup vegetable oil
1 can (6 ounces) sliced mushrooms,
undrained
½ cup cocktail peanuts
½ cup green pepper, minced

2 tablespoons cornstarch
1 large clove garlic, minced
⅛ teaspoon ground ginger
dash cayenne
¼ cup molasses
¼ cup soy sauce
¼ cup sherry

1. Cut chicken into 1-inch pieces.
2. Heat oil in skillet or wok; add chicken and brown.
3. Add undrained mushrooms, peanuts, green pepper, cornstarch, garlic, ginger, cayenne, molasses and soy sauce; cook and stir until thickened.
4. Cover and cook over low heat 10 minutes, stirring occasionally.
5. Add sherry and cook 1 minute longer.

Chicken & Vegetables Oriental

Serves 4

2 whole chicken breasts (about
12 ounces each)
¼ cup soy sauce
¼ cup chicken broth
4 tablespoons peanut oil
1 clove garlic, quartered

2 small yellow squash, with ends
removed and sliced
1 medium-size zucchini, with ends
removed and sliced
1 package (6 ounces) frozen Chinese
pea pods, thawed

½ pound mushrooms, sliced

1. Skin and bone chicken breasts; cut meat into bite-size pieces and place in glass bowl or shallow dish.
2. Mix together soy sauce and chicken broth; pour over chicken pieces, stirring to coat; marinate 1 hour (or longer).
3. Heat 2 tablespoons peanut oil in large skillet or wok until sizzling; add garlic and cook 2 minutes.
4. Remove and discard garlic pieces.
5. Remove chicken from soy mixture, reserving soy mixture; drain chicken on paper towels.
6. Cook chicken quickly in hot garlic oil, stirring constantly.
7. Remove chicken; keep warm.
8. Add remaining oil to pan and heat. Add squash and zucchini; toss in oil to coat.
9. Push vegetables to one side. Add pea pods and mushrooms; toss to coat with oil.
10. Add chicken pieces and reserved soy sauce mixture; cover, reduce heat, and simmer 5 minutes, or until vegetables are crisp-tender.

Chicken Chan

Serves 4 or 6

2 whole chicken breasts, boned,
split and skinned (or 1 pound
boneless), cut in strips
¼ teaspoon ground ginger
2 tablespoons corn oil
1 can (10¾ ounces) condensed
cream of shrimp soup

1 cup bamboo shoots
1 tablespoon soy sauce
6 cups fresh spinach, torn in bite-
size pices (about 6 ounces)
½ cup orange sections
½ cup toasted whole almonds or
cashews

1. Cook chicken with ginger in hot oil in skillet until chicken turns white, about 5 minutes, stirring constantly.
2. Add soup, bamboo shoots and soy sauce; cook, covered, over low heat 3 minutes.
3. Add spinach; cook 3 minutes longer, or until done.
4. Stir in orange sections and almonds.
5. Serve with additional soy sauce.

Chicken Tandoori with Spiced Tomato Sauce

Serves 6

3 cleaned broiler-fryer chickens,
each weighing about 2½ pounds
1½ teaspoons freshly ground black
pepper

2 tablespoons chili powder
1 teaspoon salt
3 pints plain yogurt
Spiced Tomato Sauce

1. Split chickens in half; discard backbones. Skin chicken except for the wings. Split flesh in several places to allow penetration of flavor.
2. Place chicken halves in deep container.
3. Mix together pepper, chili powder, salt and yogurt; pour over chicken.
4. Marinate in refrigerator about 2 hours.
5. Drain well and scrape as much marinade from chicken as possible.
6. Broil about 5 inches from high heat about 25 minutes, or until done, turning once.
7. Serve with Spiced Tomato Sauce poured over and around chicken

Spiced Tomato Sauce

1½ cups tomato juice
⅓ cup butter
1½ teaspoons chili powder

1 teaspoon peppercorns
1 cinnamon stick, about 2 inches
1 teaspoon salt

1. Combine all ingredients; simmer over moderate heat about 10 minutes, stirring.
2. Strain; pour over chicken.

Chicken Chinois

Serves 6

1 (3-pound) broiler-fryer, cut in
   pieces
2 tablespoons butter or margarine
salt to taste
pepper to taste
2 cans (11 ounces each) mandarin
   orange sections
1 cup sugar

½ cup lime juice
1 teaspoon lime rind, grated
1 clove garlic, crushed
2 teaspoons ground ginger
1 teaspoon salt
2 tablespoons cornstarch
2 tablespoons almonds, sliced
2 fresh Bartlett pears

hot cooked rice

1. Put chicken pieces into shallow pan; dot with butter and sprinkle with salt and pepper.
2. Bake in preheated 375° F. oven for 1 hour, or until tender, basting twice with pan juices.
3. Meanwhile, make sauce by draining about 1 cup juice from orange sections and pouring into saucepan. Mix in sugar, lime juice, lime rind, garlic, ginger, salt and cornstarch; cook, stirring, over medium heat until sauce comes to boil and is thickened.
4. Stir in almonds and mandarin oranges; set aside.
5. When chicken is nearly done, halve, core, and slice pears; add to sauce and heat through.
6. Transfer chicken to platter and spoon sauce over chicken; serve with rice.

Emperor's Chicken Suey

Serves 4 to 6

3 tablespoons soy sauce
1 teaspoon sugar
1 teaspoon ground ginger
4 whole chicken breasts, cut in
   2-inch strips
¾ cup scallions, sliced
2 tablespoons peanut oil
2 cans (3 ounces each) broiled
   mushroom crowns, undrained

1 cup water
½ cup bamboo shoots, diced
½ cup sliced water chestnuts
½ cup cucumber, diced
1 tablespoon cornstarch mixed with
   2 tablespoons water
1 package (10 ounces) fresh spinach,
   torn into small pieces
1¼ cups dry roasted peanuts

hot cooked rice

1. Combine soy sauce, sugar and ginger; add chicken strips and ¼ cup scallions; let stand 5 minutes.
2. Heat oil in large skillet; add chicken and soy mixture, stir-frying until well browned.
3. Stir in mushroom crowns, 1 cup water, remaining ½ cup scallions, bamboo shoots, water chestnuts and cucumber; simmer over low heat about 45 minutes, or until chicken is tender.
4. Add cornstarch to chicken mixture, along with spinach and peanuts; cook 5 minutes longer. Serve with rice.

Festive Chinese Chicken

Serves 4

2 pounds chicken parts
2 tablespoons shortening
1 can (10¾ ounces) condensed
    chicken broth
1 medium clove garlic, peeled
    and minced
1 tablespoon soy sauce

½ teaspoon ground ginger
4 medium carrots, cut diagonally
    in very thin slices
1 package (6 ounces) frozen
    pea pods
¼ cup water
2 tablespoons cornstarch

hot cooked rice

1. Brown chicken in shortening in skillet; pour off fat.
2. Stir in broth, garlic, soy sauce and ginger; cover and cook over low heat 35 minutes.
3. Add carrots; cook 10 minutes longer, or until done, stirring occasionally.
4. Add pea pods.
5. Gradually blend water into cornstarch until smooth; slowly stir into sauce and cook, stirring, until thickened.
6. Serve with rice and additional soy sauce.

Easy Walnut Chicken Stir-Fry

Serves 4

3 tablespoons soy sauce
1 tablespoon dry sherry
½ teaspoon ground ginger
1 pound skinned boneless chicken
    breasts, cut into 1-inch pieces
1 cup large pieces California
    walnuts

3 tablespoons corn oil
1 large garlic clove, slightly
    crushed
½ cup onion, sliced
1 large green pepper, cut into
    1-inch cubes

1. Mix together soy sauce, sherry and ginger; marinate chicken in mixture 15 minutes.
2. Meanwhile, in large skillet, toast walnuts in 1 teaspoon oil over low heat about 5 minutes, stirring frequently; remove and set aside.
3. Heat 1 tablespoon oil in skillet; stir-fry garlic and onion over moderately-high heat 2 minutes.
4. Add green pepper; continue cooking 2 minutes or less.
5. Discard garlic; remove vegetables from skillet.
6. Heat remaining oil; add chicken and marinade, stir-frying over moderately-high heat for 5 minutes.
7. Return vegetables to skillet with chicken; cook 30 seconds longer, just to heat vegetables through.
8. Add walnuts and serve.

Himalayan Chicken Curry with Rice

Serves 8

2 broiler-fryers, quartered
salt
freshly ground black pepper
3 tablespoons ghee or melted
  butter
1 cup onion, chopped
5 slices bacon, minced, or ¼ cup
  ham cut in thin julienne strips
3 tablespoons flour

1 tablespoon curry powder
2 cups chicken broth
¼ cup orange marmalade or
  mango chutney
2 tablespoons tomato purée
2 tablespoons lemon juice
6 cups hot cooked rice
ginger pear preserves
  (optional garnish)

1. Pat chicken dry; season with salt and pepper.
2. Dip quarters in ghee or melted butter; place in baking dish, skin-side up and bake in preheated 400° F. oven for 30 minutes.
3. Sauté onion and bacon until onion is tender; blend in flour and curry powder.
4. Stir in broth and cook, stirring constantly, until thickened.
5. Blend in marmalade, tomato purée and lemon juice.
6. Spoon sauce over chicken and continue baking 20 minutes longer, or until chicken is tender and richly glazed.
7. Serve chicken and sauce over bed of hot fluffy rice. (Ginger pear preserves make a beautiful garnish.)

Sambal Goreng
(Spiced Chicken with Vegetables)

Serves 6

2 teaspoons salt
1 teaspoon sugar
¼ teaspoon fresh ginger root,
  minced
¼ teaspoon cayenne pepper
2 tablespoons soy sauce
2 cloves garlic, minced
2 cups chicken, cubed

5 tablespoons peanut oil
2 cups fresh broccoli, diagonally
  cut into 2 x ½-inch slices
2 cups fresh mushrooms, sliced
1 medium onion, peeled and
  thinly sliced
4 cups hot cooked rice
½ cup water

1. Combine 1 teaspoon salt, sugar, ginger, cayenne, soy sauce and garlic in a bowl; blend well.
2. Add chicken and let marinate for 20 minutes, stirring occasionally.
3. Heat 2 tablespoons oil in wok or large skillet over high heat; add marinated chicken mixture and stir-fry 5 minutes.
4. Remove from wok; set aside.
5. Heat remaining 3 tablespoons oil; add broccoli. Sprinkle with remaining 1 teaspoon salt and stir-fry about 5 minutes.
6. Add mushrooms and onions; stir-fry until mixture is tender-crisp.
7. Return chicken to wok; add cooked rice and water, stirring until thoroughly hot.

Ground Turkey Taipei

Serves 4

1 large fresh pineapple	1 egg
2 tablespoons scallions, sliced	¾ teaspoon salt
2 tablespoons butter	2 tablespoons corn oil
½ cup green pepper, chunked	1 cup dairy sour cream
1 cup fresh mushrooms, sliced	½ teaspoon horseradish
¾ pound ground turkey	½ teaspoon basil
2 tablespoons wheat germ	1 jar (2 ounces) pimiento, sliced

1. Cut pineapple (with leaves on) in half lengthwise through crown. Cut out fruit, leaving shells intact; cut fruit into ½-inch pieces and set aside.
2. Sauté scallions in 1 tablespoon butter in large fry pan; drain on paper towels.
3. Add remaining butter and green pepper pieces to pan; sauté lightly, then drain.
4. Sauté mushrooms in same pan; drain.
5. Mix turkey with wheat germ, egg and ½ teaspoon salt; form into 1-inch balls and brown well in hot oil until cooked through.
6. Combine sour cream, horseradish, scallions, basil and remaining ¼ teaspoon salt in small saucepan; heat, but do not boil.
7. Combine meatballs, pineapple, green pepper, mushrooms and pimiento; gently fold in sauce.
8. Turn mixture into pineapple shells; cover leaves with aluminum foil and bake at 350° F. for 15 minutes, or until heated through.

Hop Po Gai Ding
(Chicken with Walnuts)

Serves 3 to 4

3 tablespoons soy sauce	½ teaspoon ground ginger
1 teaspoon sugar	2 cloves garlic, crushed
1 teaspoon salt	1 cup water
1 (3-pound) broiler-fryer	1 tablespoon cornstarch
¼ cup peanut oil	1 can (5 ounces) sliced bamboo
1 cup California walnuts	shoots

hot cooked rice

1. In a large bowl, combine soy sauce, sugar and salt.
2. Skin uncooked chicken and cut meat into bite-size pieces; add chicken to soy mixture and marinate for 20 minutes.
3. In a large skillet, heat peanut oil; add walnuts and sauté about 2 minutes.
4. Remove walnuts from skillet and set aside.
5. To remaining oil in skillet, add ginger, garlic, chicken pieces and any remaining soy sauce marinade; sauté until chicken pieces are well browned on all sides.
6. Combine water and cornstarch; add to chicken. Cover and simmer about 20 minutes.
7. Add undrained can of bamboo shoots and reserved walnuts; simmer additional 10 minutes.
8. Serve over beds of rice.

Imperial Chicken Suey

Serves 4 to 6

3 tablespoons soy sauce
1 teaspoon sugar
1 teaspoon ground ginger
2 whole chicken breasts, boned, skinned and cut in 2-inch strips
2 tablespoons peanut oil
1 can (6 ounces) broiled mushrooms, drained
1 cup plus 2 tablespoons water

¾ cup scallions, sliced
½ cup bamboo shoots, diced
½ cup water chestnuts, sliced
½ cup cucumbers, diced
1 tablespoon cornstarch
1 package (10 ounces) fresh spinach
1 cup dry roasted peanuts
hot cooked rice

1. Combine soy sauce, sugar and ginger; mix in chicken and let stand 5 minutes.
2. Heat peanut oil in large skillet over high heat; add chicken and soy sauce mixture, stir-frying until chicken is well browned.
3. Stir in mushrooms, 1 cup water, scallions, bamboo shoots, water chestnuts and cucumber; cover and simmer for 5 minutes.
4. Blend remaining 2 tablespoons water with cornstarch; stir into chicken mixture.
5. Add spinach; cover and cook 5 minutes longer.
6. Stir in peanuts; serve with hot cooked rice.

Sherried Chinese Chicken Casserole

Serves 4

2 whole chicken breasts, cut in thin strips
2 tablespoons peanut or salad oil
1½ cups fresh green beans, thinly sliced lengthwise, French-style
¼ teaspoon ground ginger
1½ cups carrots, sliced paper-thin, diagonally
1½ cups sliced fresh mushrooms
2 tablespoons sherry

1 can (10¾ ounces) condensed chicken broth
3 teaspoons cornstarch mixed with 2 tablespoons water
salt to taste
freshly ground pepper to taste
1 tablespoon soy sauce
3 cups cooked hot rice
2 tablespoons toasted slivered almonds (optional garnish)

1. Stir-fry chicken strips in hot oil in wok or skillet about 2 minutes.
2. Add green beans and ginger; cook 2 minutes, stirring constantly.
3. Add carrots; cook 10 minutes.
4. Add mushrooms; barely heat.
5. Add sherry, chicken broth, cornstarch mixture, salt, pepper and soy sauce; cook and stir until thickened and smooth.
6. Place hot rice in heated serving casserole; spoon chicken-vegetable mixture over all.
7. If desired, garnish with toasted almond slivers.

VARIATION: Substitute paper-thin strips of tender cut steak for chicken, and beef broth for chicken broth. Bamboo shoots, slivered water chestnuts or chopped spinach also make a good change of pace.

Moo Goo Gai Pan

Serves 4

2 whole skinned, boned chicken
breasts (1½ pounds)
4 tablespoons soy sauce
⅛ teaspoon ground white pepper
3 tablespoons cornstarch
1 cup chicken broth
1 can (16 ounces) chow mein
vegetables

2 tablespoons corn oil
¼ pound fresh mushrooms,
washed, pat-dried, trimmed
and sliced
2 tablespoons pimiento, sliced
¼ cup green pepper, cut in
⅛-inch slices

1. Slice chicken horizontally ¼ inch thick; cut into 1-inch squares.
2. Sprinkle with 2 tablespoons soy sauce, white pepper and 1 tablespoon cornstarch.
3. Mix together chicken broth, remaining soy sauce and remaining cornstarch in small mixing bowl; set aside.
4. Drain chow mein vegetables; set aside.
5. When ready to serve, heat oil in wok or skillet; add chicken and stir-fry 3 to 4 minutes, or until opaque.
6. Stir in mushrooms, pimiento and green pepper.
7. Stir in chicken broth mixture and stir constantly until mixture thickens.
8. Add chow mein vegetables; heat through.

Stir-Fried Chicken & Peppers

Serves 4 to 6

1 tablespoon soy sauce
1 tablespoon dry sherry
1 teaspoon fresh ginger root, minced
1 large chicken breast, boned,
skinned and cut into ½-inch cubes
4 tablespoons peanut oil
2 green peppers, cut into ½-inch
pieces

½ teaspoon salt
4 scallions, cut into ½-inch
slices
1 clove garlic, crushed
½ cup chicken broth
1 teaspoon cornstarch
1 tablespoon water
3 cups hot cooked rice

1. Blend together soy sauce, sherry and ginger in small bowl; add chicken and marinate 10 minutes.
2. Heat 2 tablespoons peanut oil in wok or large skillet over high heat; add green peppers and stir-fry 2 minutes.
3. Sprinkle peppers with salt; add scallions and stir-fry 1 minute.
4. Remove vegetables from wok and set aside.
5. Heat remaining peanut oil; add garlic and marinated chicken; stir-fry 2 to 3 minutes, or until the chicken turns white and becomes firm.
6. Return vegetables to wok; stir in chicken broth.
7. Combine cornstarch and water until smooth; stir into chicken and vegetables; cook, stirring constantly, until slightly thickened.
8. Serve at once with hot cooked rice.

Teriyaki Barbecued Chicken

Serves 2 to 3

1 broiler-fryer chicken,
  cut into serving pieces

about 1 cup teriyaki sauce

1. Place chicken pieces in shallow glass casserole.
2. Pour teriyaki sauce over chicken pieces, marinate chicken pieces 1 to 2 hours in teriyaki sauce, or overnight, turning occasionally.
3. Arrange chicken pieces on rack in shallow baking pan; bake in preheated 325° F. oven about 1 hour, turning and basting with sauce.

Holiday Duckling Stuffed with Apricots

Serves 6

1 can (30 ounces) apricot halves,
  undrained
¼ cup butter or margarine
1 cup onion, chopped
1 teaspoon soy sauce
⅛ teaspoon pepper
¼ teaspoon ground ginger
3 cups cooked brown rice
½ cup dark seedless raisins

½ cup wheat germ
⅔ cup toasted almonds, slivered
5-pound ready-to-cook duckling
1 cup water
4 teaspoons cornstarch
2 chicken bouillon cubes, dissolved
¼ cup hot water
¼ cup apricot brandy or sake
parsley sprigs

1. Drain apricots, reserving 1 cup of syrup for sauce. Set aside 8 apricot halves for garnish; dice remaining halves for stuffing.
2. Melt butter in large skillet; add onion and sauté until golden.
3. Remove from heat; stir in soy sauce and pepper.
4. Add rice, raisins, wheat germ, almonds and diced apricots; toss lightly.
5. Fill duckling with stuffing; close openings with heavy thread or poultry pins. Prick skin of breast, legs and thighs.
6. Place duckling, breast-side up, on rack in shallow roasting pan; bake duckling in preheated 425° F. oven for 20 minutes.
7. Reduce heat to 350° F. and roast 1½ to 1¾ hours longer, pouring off fat from pan twice during roasting period.
8. Place duck on serving platter, remove thread or poultry pins, and pour off and discard all fat from roasting pan.
9. Blend water with cornstarch; pour into roasting pan with reserved 1 cup apricot syrup and chicken bouillon.
10. Bring mixture to a boil over medium heat, stirring constantly; simmer 1 minute, or until brown bits are loosened from bottom of pan.
11. Strain mixture through sieve into small saucepan (there should be about 1⅓ cups); add brandy and stir just until mixture comes to a boil.
12. Taste to correct seasonings.
13. Add 8 reserved apricots; cook to heat through.
14. Remove apricots with slotted spoon and place around duck for garnish with parsley sprigs. Brush duck with sauce; pass remaining sauce to serve with duck.

Turkey Oriental

Serves 6

1 package (10 ounces) frozen
   broccoli spears, cooked and
   drained
1½ cups celery, diagonally sliced
⅛ teaspoon ground ginger
2 tablespoons butter or margarine
2 cups cooked turkey, cubed

2 cans (10½ ounces each) chicken
   giblet gravy
1 package (6 ounces) snow peas,
   cooked and drained
½ cup water chestnuts, sliced
1 tablespoon soy sauce
cooked rice

1. Cut broccoli spears in 1-inch pieces; set aside.
2. Cook celery with ginger in butter in skillet until tender.
3. Add broccoli and remaining ingredients except rice; heat, stirring occasionally.
4. Serve over hot cooked rice.

NOTE: *Snow peas can be replaced with 1 cup carrots, thinly sliced diagonally, and cooked with celery.*

Chinese Chunks of Duckling
with Canton Sauce

Serves 6

1 (5-pound) cleaned, ready-to-cook
   duckling, cut into pieces
water
¼ cup scallions, sliced
⅛ teaspoon pepper
3 tablespoons soy sauce
¼ cup cornstarch
1 can (6 ounces) sliced mushrooms,
   drained

3 eggs, beaten
1 cup unsifted all-purpose flour
½ teaspoon salt
peanut oil
4 cups lettuce, shredded
¼ cup toasted blanched almonds
   chopped (for garnish)

1. Place duckling pieces in large saucepan; cover with cold water and bring to a boil.
2. Reduce heat and simmer about 50 minutes, or until tender.
3. Drain duckling and set aside; reserve 2 cups strained, fat-free, broth.
4. In small saucepan, combine reserved broth, scallions, pepper and soy sauce. Bring to a boil, reduce heat, and simmer 3 minutes.
5. Meanwhile, blend together cornstarch and 3 tablespoons water until smooth; stir into simmering mixture.
6. Add mushrooms and heat until clear; set aside and keep warm.
7. Combine beaten eggs, ½ cup water, flour and salt; beat batter until smooth.
8. Remove meat from duckling bones in large sections, discard skin, and cut into bite-size pieces.
9. Dip chunks of duckling into batter; drop individual pieces, a few at a time, into deep hot peanut oil heated to 375° F. Fry until crisp and lightly browned.
10. Drain on absorbent paper.
11. Make a border of lettuce around the edge of a platter; arrange duckling chunks in center. Pour on hot mushroom sauce and garnish with almonds.

Crab & Vegetables Mikado

Serves 6

6 to 8 ounces frozen Alaska King
  crabmeat
¼ pound fresh mushrooms
2 tablespoons butter
1 can (6 ounces) bamboo shoots
1 can (1 pound) bean sprouts

4 scallions, sliced in 1½-inch
  slices
¼ cup soy sauce
4 teaspoons sugar
1 tablespoon vinegar
hot steamed rice

1. Thaw and drain crab; slice into chunks.
2. If mushrooms are large, slice; sauté in butter until golden.
3. Add crab and remaining ingredients to mushrooms; simmer until heated, stirring gently.
4. Serve with hot rice.

Chu's Dragon Fish
with Sweet & Sour Sauce

Serves 4

1 cleaned whole rock cod, weighing
  3 to 4 pounds
hot water
1 cup flour
6 cups oil

Sweet & Sour Sauce
6 sliced lemons (for garnish)
½ cup Chinese pickled mixed vegetables (available at Chinese
  markets) (for garnish)

1. Remove fish head and set aside.
2. Fillet fish by cutting along the back with a sharp knife; then cut down the spine and over the ribs, stopping just short of the tail.
3. Turn fish over; fillet the other side the same way.
4. Cut out the bones with kitchen shears or with a heavy knife on a chopping board.
5. Lay fillets skin-side down and score the meat just to the skin in a diamond pattern.
6. Dip the scored fish in hot water for a few seconds to accentuate the pattern; pat-dry and dredge fish in flour.
7. Heat oil to 350° F. in wok or deep kettle so it is 4 inches deep; holding the fish back to back, immerse it in the oil and fry it until it is browned, about 5 to 7 minutes. (You may also fry the floured fish head for garnish.)
8. Serve fish coated with heated Sweet & Sour Sauce, decorated with lemon slices and pickled vegetables.

Sweet & Sour Sauce

1 cup water
½ cup sugar
½ cup white vinegar
½ cup catsup

salt
juice of ¼ lemon
2 tablespoons cornstarch
2 tablespoons water

1. Combine water, sugar, vinegar, catsup, salt and lemon juice in saucepan.
2. Bring to a boil and thicken with paste made from cornstarch and water.

Floundering Cakes

Serves 4 to 5

1 tablespoon cornstarch
1 tablespoon soy sauce
3 cups cooked, flaked flounder
¾ cup ground blanched almonds
½ cup scallions, minced

1 egg, beaten
2 tablespoons fresh parsley,
  chopped, or fresh Chinese parsley
  (sold in Chinese groceries)
½ teaspoon salt
peanut oil

1. Mix cornstarch with soy sauce.
2. Combine flounder, almonds, scallions, egg, parsley and salt; add in cornstarch mixture and mix until well blended.
3. Form into 10 patties; pan-fry in hot oil until brown on both sides.

NOTE: *Good as first course or as entrée.*

Halibut Hong Kong

Serves 6

2 pounds halibut steaks, fresh
  or frozen
¼ cup soy sauce
¼ cup frozen orange juice concen-
  trate, thawed

2 tablespoons catsup
2 tablespoons corn oil
1 tablespoon fresh lemon juice
¼ teaspoon pepper
1 clove garlic, mashed

1. Thaw frozen steaks; place in single layer in shallow baking pan.
2. Combine remaining ingredients; mix well.
3. Pour marinade mixture over halibut; let stand 1 hour, turning once.
4. Drain off marinade and reserve.
5. Broil halibut about 4 inches from source of heat for 10 to 15 minutes, or until fish flakes easily when tested with a fork.
6. Baste with marinade during broiling.
7. Serve immediately.

Japanese Scallops in Sake

Serves 2 to 3

1 pound scallops
½ teaspoon salt
2 tablespoons sake
1 tablespoon olive oil

1 tablespoon fresh lemon juice
pinch each: paprika, white pepper
  and dried parsley
1 tablespoon butter or oil

1. Wash and dry scallops.
2. Mix remaining ingredients except butter.
3. Marinate scallops in mixture at least 15 minutes.
4. Heat butter in electric fry pan; sauté scallops on both sides until golden.

Lobster with Black Bean Sauce

Serves 4

2 pounds frozen spiny lobster tails
4 teaspoons fermented black beans
  (available in Chinese groceries)
4 cloves garlic, peeled
2 teaspoons fresh ginger, minced
4 tablespoons soy sauce
1 teaspoon honey

4 tablespoons peanut oil
4 tablespoons ground pork
2/3 cup boiling water
4 teaspoons cornstarch mixed with
  1 tablespoon water
4 tablespoons green pepper, minced
2 eggs, slightly beaten

1. Thaw frozen lobster tails; cut away and remove undershells. If 6 ounces or larger, split through shell lengthwise.
2. Wash black beans thoroughly in cold running water; drain.
3. Crush black beans with 1 garlic clove; mix in ginger, soy sauce and honey; heat oil over high heat in a wok.
4. Add remaining whole garlic cloves and pork; brown quickly. Lift out and discard garlic.
5. Add lobster and boiling water; spoon black bean mixture over lobster flesh. Cover and cook over medium heat 6 minutes.
6. Add cornstarch paste; heat and stir until it coats lobster.
7. Add green pepper and eggs; heat and stir until eggs set. Serve immediately.

NOTE: Great dish for garlic lovers! For Cantonese cooks, garlic invariably goes with ginger and fermented black beans (also called preserved black beans).

Shrimp Chow Mein

Serves 4

3 tablespoons corn oil
2 pounds fresh shrimp, shelled
  and deveined, or 1 pound frozen
  cleaned shrimp (partially thawed)
1 clove garlic, peeled and minced
6 mushrooms, sliced
1½ cups celery, diagonally sliced

½ cup drained bean sprouts
¼ cup bamboo shoots, sliced
1 cup chicken broth
1 teaspoon salt
2 tablespoons cornstarch
½ cup water
1 teaspoon soy sauce

chow mein noodles or hot rice

1. Heat corn oil in large skillet over medium heat; add shrimp and garlic; sauté, stirring occasionally, 3 minutes.
2. Stir in mushrooms, celery, bean sprouts, bamboo shoots, broth and salt; cook over medium heat 3 minutes.
3. Stir together cornstarch, water and soy sauce until smooth; stir into vegetable mixture.
4. Bring to a boil, stirring constantly, over medium heat; boil 1 minute.
5. Serve with chow mein noodles or rice.

Rainbow Trout with Chinese Black Bean Sauce

Serves 2

4 small, whole dressed rainbow
   trout, fresh or frozen
salt
freshly ground black pepper
¼ cup butter, melted
2 teaspoons cornstarch
1 teaspoon sugar
⅛ teaspoon ground ginger

¾ cup water
2 tablespoons vinegar
1 tablespoon soy sauce
1 teaspoon instant chicken bouillon
1 clove garlic, crushed
½ cup black beans or pinto beans,
   drained

1. Thaw trout if frozen; wash and dry. Season cavity with salt and pepper. Make several diagonal slashes on each fish about 1½ inches apart.
2. Place trout in baking dish and drizzle with melted butter; bake in a preheated 450° F. oven 20 minutes, or until fish flakes easily when tested with a fork. (Start checking trout for doneness about 5 minutes before recommended finish time. DO NOT OVERCOOK!)
3. While fish bakes prepare the sauce: in small saucepan, combine cornstarch, sugar and ginger; gradually blend in water until smooth.
4. Stir in vinegar, soy sauce, bouillon, garlic, ⅛ teaspoon pepper and beans; bring sauce to a boil over medium heat while stirring constantly; continue to boil 2 minutes.
5. Serve sauce over baked fish.

Shrimp Curry

Serves 4 to 6

1 cup celery, diced
¼ cup onion, chopped
¼ cup butter
5 tablespoons flour
1 teaspoon salt
1 teaspoon curry powder
½ teaspoon sugar
⅛ teaspoon ground ginger
2 chicken bouillon cubes

2 cups hot water
1 pound cooked shrimp, drained
   and deveined
½ teaspoon lemon juice
2 tablespoons dry sherry
hot cooked rice
condiments: chopped peanuts, coconut,
   chopped hard-cooked egg, crisp
   crumbled bacon, chutney, raisins

1. In 1½-quart casserole, combine celery, onions and butter; cover and cook 6 to 7 minutes, or until onions and celery are limp.
2. Stir in flour, salt, curry powder, sugar and ginger; cover and cook 1 minute.
3. Dissolve bouillon cubes in hot water; gradually add bouillon to flour mixture, stirring until smooth. Cover and cook 5 to 7 minutes until thickened and smooth, stirring occasionally.
4. Add shrimp and lemon juice; cover and heat 2 to 3 minutes.
5. Stir in sherry; serve over hot rice with condiments.

Sweet & Pungent Shrimp

Serves 4 to 6

1 medium onion, quartered
1 cup celery, diagonally sliced
2 tablespoons salad oil
⅔ cup firmly packed brown sugar
2 tablespoons cornstarch
½ teaspoon salt
⅛ teaspoon ground ginger
⅓ cup vinegar

3 tablespoons soy sauce
1 can (6 ounces) pineapple juice
1¼ cups water
2 cups fresh pineapple, cubed
1 pound cooked, cleaned shrimp
   (preferably fresh)
1 green pepper, cut into
   1-inch pieces

hot cooked rice

1. Sauté onion and celery in hot oil; set aside.
2. Combine sugar, cornstarch, salt and ginger; stir in vinegar and soy sauce.
3. Add vinegar mixture, pineapple juice and water to vegetables; cook, stirring constantly, until thickened and clear.
4. Add pineapple, shrimp and green pepper; cover and continue cooking 5 minutes.
5. Serve with bowl of rice alongside!

NOTE: *Fun to serve in pineapple shell, if desired!*

Shrimp Canton

Serves 4 to 5

1 pound frozen shrimp, thawed,
   cleaned and deveined
¼ cup soy sauce
¼ cup water
2 teaspoons sugar
2 tablespoons butter or margarine

1 teaspoon ground ginger
1 large green pepper, cut into
   1-inch squares
¼ pound large mushrooms, sliced
18 to 20 cherry tomatoes
hot cooked rice

1. Drain and dry shrimp well on paper towels.
2. Marinate for ½ hour in mixture of soy sauce, water and sugar.
3. Melt butter in large fry pan; stir in ginger.
4. Add green pepper and cook about 3 minutes.
5. Add mushrooms and shrimp mixture; bring to a slow boil and cook about 8 minutes.
6. Add tomatoes and cook 3 minutes longer.
7. Serve over rice.

Shrimp Vindaloo

Serves 6

½ teaspoon powdered mustard
½ teaspoon warm water
½ cup white vinegar
2 tablespoons curry powder
2 tablespoons onion powder
2 teaspoons garlic powder
1½ teaspoons ground ginger

1 teaspoon salt
1/16 teaspoon ground red pepper
2 pounds large raw shrimp,
  peeled and deveined
2 tablespoons butter or margarine
¼ cup boiling water
hot cooked rice (optional)

1. In a cup, combine mustard with warm water; let stand 10 minutes for flavor to develop.
2. In large bowl, blend vinegar with mustard, curry, onion and garlic powders, ginger, salt and red pepper; mix well.
3. Add shrimp to vinegar mixture, coating shrimp on all sides; cover and refrigerate at least 12 hours.
4. When ready to serve, melt butter in large skillet; add shrimp and fry about 2 minutes, stirring constantly.
5. Remove skillet from heat; add boiling water and cook 4 minutes longer, or until shrimp are done.
6. Serve with rice, if desired.

Fried Rock Lobster with Subgum Sauce

Serves 6

24 ounces frozen South African
  rock lobster tails, defrosted
3 tablespoons peanut oil
½ clove garlic, mashed
1 teaspoon salt
1 tablespoon soy sauce
2 cans (3 ounces each) sliced
  mushrooms, with liquid

1 cup scallions, sliced
1 cup celery, sliced
1 green pepper, cut in strips
½ cup water chestnuts, sliced
½ cup bamboo shoots, sliced
1 tablespoon cornstarch
1 cup chicken broth or stock
hot cooked rice

crisp Chinese noodles

1. Cut away underside membrane and remove raw rock lobster meat from shells; cut meat into large chunks.
2. Heat peanut oil in large skillet; add rock lobster, garlic and salt; sauté rapidly until rock lobster meat turns creamy white, about 1 to 2 minutes.
3. Add soy sauce and all the vegetables.
4. Blend cornstarch with small amount of chicken broth; add to remaining chicken broth.
5. Add broth mixture to skillet; cook over low heat until vegetables are tender-crisp and sauce is smooth and thickened, about 5 minutes.
6. Serve over hot cooked rice and crisp noodles with additional soy sauce.

Singing Fish Stew

Serves 3 to 4

4 cups water or clam juice
1 onion, peeled and sliced
juice of 1 lemon
12 red radishes, cleaned and
   chopped, or daikon (Japanese
   radish), slivered
1 cucumber, peeled and sliced

1 red pepper, seeded and quartered
1 pound whitefish, haddock or
   cod, cut in 2-inch pieces
3 tomatoes, peeled and chopped
sea salt to taste
soy sauce (optional)
hot cooked rice (optional)

1. Bring water or clam juice to a boil; add onion, lemon juice, chopped radishes, cucumber and pepper. Cook until vegetables begin to get tender.
2. Add fish and tomatoes; simmer about 8 minutes, or until fish is just beginning to flake.
3. Season to taste. Serve hot with soy sauce or with rice.

NOTE: Wonderful to use freshly caught fish (freshwater or saltwater).

Mandarin Sweet 'n' Sour Rock Lobster with Pineapple

Serves 6

6 (4 ounces each) frozen South
   African rock lobster tails
4 tablespoons peanut oil
4 scallions, diced
5 water chestnuts, thinly sliced
½ green pepper, cut in strips
1 cup pineapple cubes, well drained

¼ cup sweet pickles, sliced
½ cup pineapple juice
1 tablespoon cider vinegar
1 tablespoon grated ginger root
   (juice and pulp)
1 tablespoon cornstarch moistened
   with water

hot cooked rice

1. Parboil lobster tails by dropping in boiling salted water; when water reboils, cook 1 minute.
2. Drain immediately and drench with cold water.
3. Cut away thin underside membrane and remove meat from shells; cut each tail into 5 or 6 pieces and set aside.
4. Heat oil in heavy skillet; add scallions, water chestnuts and green pepper; sauté lightly.
5. Add pineapple cubes and pickles.
6. Mix together pineapple juice, vinegar and ginger; add to vegetable-pineapple mixture and simmer all together for a few minutes.
7. Stir in cornstarch, cook until thickened.
8. Add lobster pieces to sauce, bring back to a boil, and cook in sauce for 4 minutes.
9. Serve immediately with rice.

Taka-Yaki, House of Sue Ouchi
(Crab-Tofu Omelet)

Serves 3 to 4

10 ounces tofu, well drained
and crushed
3 dried Oriental mushroom caps,
softened in warm water, drained
and finely sliced
1 can (6 ounces) crabmeat, gristle-
free and finely minced

3 eggs, beaten together
1 teaspoon mirin
⅓ teaspoon soy sauce
1 teaspoon flour
1 tablespoon green peas, canned,
or frozen and thawed, or fresh
and lightly cooked

1 tablespoon vegetable oil

1. Mix together tofu, mushrooms, crabmeat, eggs, mirin, soy sauce, flour and green peas.
2. Heat oil and pour half the mixture into skillet; cover and cook over low heat until set. Repeat using remaining ingredients.
3. Slice into 1 x 2-inch pieces. Serve hot with additional soy sauce.

NOTE: Can be made with shrimp, ham or minced chicken in lieu of crabmeat. In Japan, this simple but delicious omelet is served at breakfast, or with meat or fish dishes. For Westerners, it makes an interesting brunch or supper dish.

Rock Lobster Chow Mein

Serves 6

24 ounces frozen South African
rock lobster tails
¼ cup corn oil
¼ cup celery leaves, minced
½ cup onion, minced
1 can (number 2) bean sprouts
1 can (3 ounces) sliced mushrooms
1½ cups water

1 cup celery, minced
¼ cup flour
2 teaspoons sugar
1½ teaspoons salt
1 to 3 tablespoons soy sauce
1 can (number 2½) Chinese noodles
2 hard-cooked eggs, sliced
(for garnish)

1. Drop frozen lobster tails into boiling salted water; when water reboils, cook for 2 to 3 minutes.
2. Drain immediately and drench with cold water.
3. Cut away underside membrane and remove meat from shells; cube lobster and set aside.
4. Heat oil in skillet; add celery leaves and onion; cook until yellow.
5. Drain bean sprouts and mushrooms, reserving liquid; add drained liquid, 1 cup water and celery to skillet mixture; cover and simmer 15 minutes.
6. Mix flour to a smooth paste with remaining ½ cup water; stir into hot mixture.
7. Add sugar, salt and soy sauce to taste.
8. Add lobster cubes; cover and simmer over low heat about 5 minutes, or until thoroughly heated.
9. Serve over noodles; garnish with sliced hard-cooked eggs.

Rock Lobster Kyoto

Serves 6

6 (3 to 5 ounces each) frozen South
African rock lobster tails, thawed
¼ cup corn oil
1½ cups celery, diagonally sliced
1 cup peas, fresh or frozen
4 carrots, peeled and sliced
diagonally

2 cups cabbage, shredded
6 scallions, cut into ½-inch
slices
1 teaspoon sugar
2 tablespoons soy sauce
1 cup chicken broth
hot cooked rice

1. With scissors, cut away thin underside membrane of rock lobster tails; remove meat and cut into 1-inch slices.
2. Heat oil in large heavy skillet; add vegetables. Stir and sauté over medium heat for 5 minutes.
3. Add lobster meat and remaining ingredients, except rice; simmer for additional 10 minutes.
4. Serve with hot cooked rice.

Stir-Fried Rock Lobster, House of Liu

Serves 6

24 ounces frozen South African
rock lobster tails, thawed
⅓ cup peanut oil
1½ cups celery, sliced
1½ cups fresh or frozen peas
1½ cups Chinese cabbage, shredded

6 scallions, cut into 1-inch lengths
1 teaspoon sugar
1 teaspoon salt
2 tablespoons soy sauce
1½ cups chicken stock
½ clove garlic, mashed

hot cooked rice

1. With scissors, cut away underside membrane, remove raw meat, and cut into ½-inch crosswise slices.
2. Heat peanut oil in large skillet; sauté lobster pieces and vegetables, stirring constantly over high heat for 10 minutes.
3. Add remaining ingredients except rice; cover and simmer for 5 minutes, or until vegetables are tender but still crisp.
4. Serve with rice.

Salmon Teriyaki

Serves 4 to 5

1½ pounds salmon fillets or
steaks, 1 inch thick

¼ cup teriyaki barbecue marinade
and sauce

1 lemon, cut into wedges

1. Arrange salmon pieces, side by side, in small shallow pan; pour teriyaki sauce over salmon, turning pieces several times to coat both sides.
2. Marinate fish 30 minutes, turning over once.
3. Remove from marinade and place on rack of broiler pan; broil 5 to 7 minutes, or until fish flakes when tested with fork. Serve immediately with lemon wedges.

Gingered Shrimp Oriental

Serves 6

¼ cup cornstarch
2 teaspoons sugar
1 teaspoon ground ginger
1 cup dry sherry
½ cup soy sauce
½ cup water
1 pound fresh or frozen, peeled
    and deveined shrimp, thawed

½ cup onion, chopped
1 clove garlic, crushed
2 tablespoons sesame oil
1 large cucumber, forked, cut into
    ⅛-inch slices and halved
    (about 2 cups)
rice or chow mein noodles
    (optional)

1. Blend together cornstarch, sugar and ginger in small mixing bowl; gradually stir in sherry, soy sauce and water until smooth.
2. Add thawed shrimp to mixture, tossing to coat; marinate in refrigerator several hours.
3. Sauté onion and garlic in sesame oil in large skillet until tender.
4. Drain marinade from shrimp; reserve marinade.
5. Add shrimp to skillet and sauté until cooked through, about 3 to 5 minutes.
6. Add reserved marinade and heat to boiling, stirring occasionally. Boil 2 minutes.
7. Stir in cucumber and heat. Serve shrimp over rice or chow mein noodles.

Saucy Shrimp Cantonese

Serves 6 to 8

lemon or lime juice
3 or 4 avocados, halved and peeled
1 tablespoon butter or margarine
½ cup scallions, finely chopped
2 cans (3½ ounces each) shrimp,
    drained
3 tablespoons prepared mustard

3 tablespoons lemon juice
2 tablespoons soy sauce
¼ teaspoon tarragon leaves,
    crumbled
small can water chestnuts, drained
    and sliced
buttered bread crumbs

parsley or watercress (for garnish)

1. Sprinkle a few drops of lemon or lime juice on avocados to keep them from turning brown; set aside.
2. Melt butter in large skillet; add scallions and cook over low heat until limp. Remove from heat.
3. Wash shrimp; drain. Add to scallions along with mustard, lemon juice, soy sauce, tarragon and water chestnuts.
4. Place avocado shells in heatproof dish; heap shrimp mixture in each and sprinkle with buttered crumbs.
5. Broil 1 minute, or until crumbs are lightly browned.
6. Garnish with parsley or watercress.

NOTE: Fresh lobster or crabmeat works very well in this main dish favorite! For added zip, sprinkle lobster or crab with a few drops of lemon juice combined with soy sauce. Canned, drained Chinese vegetables or bamboo shoots can be substituted for water chestnuts for interesting effects.

Beef with Peppers & Tomatoes

Serves 4 to 6

¼ cup soy sauce
1 tablespoon water
1 teaspoon sherry
1½ teaspoons cornstarch
1 pound flank steak
1 clove garlic, crushed

3 tablespoons peanut oil
2½ cups green pepper, coarsely diced
1 teaspoon salt
½ teaspoon freshly ground black pepper

2 large ripe tomatoes, cut in wedges

1. Blend soy sauce, water and sherry with cornstarch.
2. Cut steak into thin slices; add to soy sauce mixture, along with garlic.
3. Heat oil in skillet; add peppers and cook over medium heat, stirring constantly, until almost tender.
4. Add beef, salt and pepper; mix well.
5. Cook until meat is tender, about 15 minutes; stir in tomatoes and continue cooking until tender.

Eggplant with Spicy Beef, House of Len

Serves 6

4 Oriental eggplants (about 1 pound)
peanut oil
1 tablespoon chile oil (available in Oriental groceries)
1 tablespoon garlic, mashed
1 cup ground pork or ½ cup ground beef and ½ cup ground pork
1 tablespoon soy sauce
¾ cup chicken broth

2 tablespoons hoisin sauce (available in supermarkets or Oriental groceries)
1 tablespoon Chinese rice vinegar
2 teaspoons cornstarch
1 teaspoon water
1 tablespoon scallions, minced (green part only)

1. Remove blossom end of eggplants. Cut in halves lengthwise; cut each half in ½-inch diagonal slices.
2. Steam eggplants until tender, or fry in 1-inch hot oil in large skillet or wok until golden brown; drain well on paper towel and set aside.
3. Drain off all oil from skillet; add chile oil and cook over high heat 30 seconds.
4. Add garlic; stir and cook 10 seconds.
5. Add ground pork, soy sauce, broth and hoisin; stir-fry until pork is browned.
6. Add vinegar and eggplants; toss lightly to blend flavors and heat eggplant through. (Add more soy sauce, if needed, to taste.)
7. Mix cornstarch with water; stir into pork mixture and cook, stirring, until ingredients glisten.
8. Add scallions; stir-fry 5 seconds. Serve at once.

NOTE: A very authentic Chinese dish! Oriental eggplants are long and slender. Use Oriental ingredients for a taste adventure you'll long remember. Also a terrific chance to use your steamer, if you haven't already!

Cantonese Grilled Steak
with Oyster Sauce

Serves 4 to 6

2 pounds sirloin steaks
small clove garlic, crushed
3 tablespoons soy sauce

2 teaspoons oyster sauce (found in
   Chinese groceries)
1 teaspoon sherry or sake

1. Trim excess fat from steaks.
2. Combine garlic, soy and oyster sauces and sherry; mix well.
3. Rub marinade carefully into both sides of steak with hands; broil 6 to 7 minutes per side in preheated broiler, or charcoal broil outdoors. Serve piping hot.

Japanese Beef & Noodle Stew

Serves 2

¼ pound round beef, cubed
1 tablespoon butter
1 package instant ramen noodles
2 tablespoons cornstarch

2 tablespoons cold water
1 tablespoon teriyaki sauce
¼ cup red wine
¼ teaspoon ground ginger

1. Brown beef in butter; set aside.
2. Prepare ramen according to package directions; drain liquid from noodles, reserving hot liquid.
3. Add cornstarch to cold water, stirring until dissolved.
4. Carefully add hot liquid from noodles to cornstarch mixture; heat until mixture becomes thick and glossy.
5. Add teriyaki sauce, wine and ginger to sauce.
6. Combine beef, noodles and sauce; mix well. Serve hot.

Korean-Style Short Ribs

Serves 4

4 pounds beef short ribs,
   2½ inches long
½ cup naturally brewed soy sauce
¼ cup water

1 tablespoon sugar
1 tablespoon sesame seed, toasted
1 teaspoon Tabasco sauce
½ teaspoon garlic powder

1. Score meaty side of ribs, opposite bone, ½ inch apart, ½ inch deep, lengthwise and crosswise.
2. Combine soy sauce, water, sugar, sesame seed, Tabasco and garlic powder; stir until sugar dissolves.
3. Place ribs and sauce in large plastic bag; press air out of bag and close top securely. Marinate 2 hours in refrigerator; turning bag over occasionally.
4. Remove ribs from marinade, and place on broiler pan; broil 2 inches from heat 15 minutes, or until ribs are brown and crispy on all sides.

Lion's Heads

Serves 5

3 large Chinese mushrooms
warm water
3 tablespoons soy sauce
2 tablespoons sherry
1 teaspoon salt
1 tablespoon sugar (optional)
1¼ pounds lean ground beef

2 scallions, chopped
½ teaspoon fresh ginger root, grated
1 tablespoon peanut oil
½ pound hearts of Chinese cabbage
  or broccoli, cut in quarters
1 cup beef broth
freshly ground pepper to taste

1. Soak mushrooms in warm water to cover for 15 minutes.
2. Drain, squeeze dry, dice in large pieces, and set aside.
3. To prepare marinade, combine soy sauce, sherry, salt and sugar; set aside.
4. Mix together diced mushrooms, beef, scallions and ginger root; form into 5 large meatballs and marinate 5 minutes in sherry-soy sauce.
5. Heat peanut oil in wok; stir-fry cabbage a few minutes, distributing greens evenly on bottom of wok to form a bed for the Lion Heads.
6. Top greens with meatballs; pour in beef broth and season to taste.
7. Cover and steam 15 minutes over low heat, until meatballs are done. Serve very hot.

NOTE: *This Shanghai classic sounds ferocious, although the dish is tame in flavor. Nonetheless, the name reveals the serio-comic attitude of Chinese cooks!*

Sukiyaki Kyoto

Serves 6

2½ pounds well-marbled sirloin
2 cups carrots, thinly sliced
2 cups celery, thinly sliced
1 cup scallions, finely chopped
1 can (8 ounces) bamboo shoots,
  drained and sliced

1 can (8½ ounces) water chestnuts,
  drained and sliced
½ tablespoon sugar
¼ cup soy or oyster sauce
1 cup beef broth or bouillon
1 tablespoon Angostura aromatic bitters

1. Cut fat from outer edge of sirloin and reserve.
2. To slice meat thinly, freeze until firm, but not hard; then cut into paper-thin strips about 1½ inches wide with very sharp knife or Chinese meat cleaver.
3. Arrange meat and all vegetables on a tray; combine remaining ingredients in a bowl.
4. Dice reserved fat and fry in a large skillet until crisp; remove crisp pieces.
5. Add meat to skillet and cook quickly over very high heat; add vegetables and cook while stirring.
6. Add liquid mixture; cover and let steam for 5 minutes, or until vegetables are tender-crisp.

Sirloin Steak Nectarine Sukiyaki

Serves 6 to 8

2 pounds sirloin steak
2 large onions
6 to 8 scallions
3 or 4 fresh nectarines
¼ pound mushrooms, sliced

1 can (5 ounces) bamboo shoots,
  drained and sliced
½ cup soy sauce
scant 2 tablespoons sugar
½ cup condensed beef broth

hot cooked rice

1. Cut steak crosswise into thin slices, saving fat.
2. Cut onions into thin wedges.
3. Slice scallions, including tops, into 2-inch lengths.
4. Slice nectarines to make 2 cups.
5. Grease skillet by rendering steak fat; remove fat and brown beef quickly.
6. Add sliced vegetables.
7. Combine soy sauce, sugar and broth; add to meat along with nectarines and simmer 5 minutes.
8. Serve over hot rice.

Beef Sukiyaki

Serves 4 to 6

2 pounds boneless beef sirloin,
  sliced as thinly as possible
4 stalks celery, sliced diagonally
  in ½-inch pieces
2 medium onions, thinly sliced
1 bunch scallions including tops,
  cut into 2-inch lengths
1 cup fresh, cleaned mushrooms, sliced
1 can (8½ ounces) bamboo shoots,
  sliced

1 can (8½ ounces) shirataki (yam
  noodles), drained (available at
  Oriental groceries)
1 block tofu, cut in 1-inch cubes
  (available in supermarkets or
  health food stores)
½ cup naturally brewed soy sauce
⅓ cup water
3 tablespoons white wine
1 tablespoon sugar

2 pieces beef suet or 1 tablespoon corn oil

1. Arrange beef and vegetables attractively on large platter.
2. Combine soy sauce, water, wine and sugar.
3. Turn electric skillet setting to 300° F. Melt suet in skillet, stirring until pan is well coated; remove browned suet. Or, heat oil in skillet.
4. Add about ⅓ of meat; cover with ½ of soy sauce mixture; add ⅔ of each vegetable, keeping meat and vegetables separate.
5. Turn ingredients over gently while cooking, 5 to 6 minutes.
6. Add another ⅓ of meat; cook an additional 1 to 2 minutes.
7. Serve sukiyaki immediately in individual bowls or plates. Replenish skillet with remaining ingredients as needed.

NOTE: For chicken sukiyaki, substitute boned and sliced chicken for beef.

Mikado's Beef with Broccoli Buds

Serves 4

1 pound lean top-beef sirloin
1 pound fresh broccoli
non-stick cooking spray

½ cup water
1 tablespoon soy sauce
1 clove garlic, pressed

1. Partially freeze beef to slice easily. Remove from freezer and cut against grain into wafer-thin strips with Chinese meat cleaver or sharp knife.
2. Trim tender buds from broccoli; cut thicker stems into thin strips lengthwise.
3. Spray a large non-stick skillet with cooking spray.
4. Add meat slices in a single layer and brown over high heat on one side only.
5. Remove meat from skillet; set aside.
6. Combine water, broccoli, soy sauce and garlic in skillet; cook over high heat, uncovered, just until broccoli is tender-crisp and most of water has evaporated.
7. Stir in meat strips; heat through. Serve hot from the skillet.

NOTE: Great for dieters – 205 calories per serving!

Cantonese Beef

Serves 6 to 8

2 pounds top round steak, cut in
  1¼-inch pieces
2 tablespoons corn oil
½ teaspoon salt
½ teaspoon ground ginger
1 medium onion, peeled and
  chopped
1½ cups water
3 tablespoons soy sauce

2 tablespoons cornstarch
2 cups celery, sliced
½ pound mushrooms, sliced
1 small green pepper, cut in strips
1 can (8 ounces) water chestnuts,
  drained
1 can (16 ounces) mandarin orange
  sections, drained

1. Brown meat in hot oil in wok or large frying pan; pour off drippings.
2. Sprinkle salt and ginger over meat.
3. Add onions, 1 cup water and soy sauce; heat to boiling.
4. Reduce heat, cover tightly, and cook slowly 1½ hours, or until meat is tender.
5. Blend ½ cup water with cornstarch; stir into meat mixture and cook, stirring constantly, until mixture thickens.
6. Stir in celery, mushrooms, green pepper and water chestnuts; continue cooking, covered, 5 to 7 minutes.
7. Add mandarin orange sections; heat through and serve.

Beef Teriyaki with Variations and Quick Sweet & Sour Sauce

Serves 4

¼ cup dark corn syrup
¼ cup soy sauce
2 tablespoons dry white wine
1 small clove garlic, crushed

½ teaspoon ground ginger or 1½ teaspoons ginger root, minced
1 to 1¼ pounds flank steak
Quick Sweet & Sour Sauce

1. Combine corn syrup, soy sauce, wine, garlic and ginger in shallow baking dish.
2. Add steak, turning to coat; cover and refrigerate, turning occasionally, several hours or overnight.
3. Remove steak from marinade; place on broiler rack and broil 6 inches from heat about 8 minutes, turning once and brushing with marinade, or until desired doneness.
4. Slice diagonally and serve immediately with Quick Sweet & Sour Sauce.

Chicken Teriyaki or Yaki-Tori (Variation)

Serves 4

1. Follow recipe for Beef Teriyaki, substituting 2 whole boned, skinned chicken breasts, cut into 1½-inch cubes, for flank steak.
2. Marinate, turning occasionally, several hours or overnight.
3. Thread chicken onto small skewers; broil 6 inches from heat about 5 minutes, turning frequently and brushing with marinade, or until chicken is tender and browned.

Fish Teriyaki (Variation)

Serves 2 to 3

1. Follow recipe for Beef Teriyaki, substituting 2 (1-inch-thick) salmon, snapper or halibut steaks for flank steak.
2. Marinate, turning occasionally, several hours or overnight.
3. Broil 6 inches from heat about 8 minutes, turning once and brushing with marinade, or until fish flakes easily.

Quick Sweet & Sour Sauce

Makes about ⅔ cup

1. In small saucepan, stir together ½ cup remaining marinade and 2 tablespoons white vinegar or lemon juice.
2. Cook over medium heat, stirring occasionally, 2 to 3 minutes, or until heated.

Stir-Fried Gingered Beef

Serves 4

1 pound flank steak
⅓ cup water
¼ cup sherry
2 tablespoons soy sauce
2 tablespoons peanut oil
1 large clove garlic, minced

1 teaspoon ginger root, shredded
3 cups radishes, sliced
1 cup scallions, diagonally sliced
1 can (10¾ ounces) condensed
   golden mushroom soup
hot cooked rice

1. Place steak in freezer for 1 hour to firm (makes slicing easier); slice diagonally across grain into thin slices with sharp knife or meat cleaver.
2. Combine water, sherry and soy sauce; add steak and marinate 1 hour.
3. Pour oil in electric wok and preheat, uncovered, at medium heat about 2 minutes.
4. Add steak, marinade, garlic and ginger; cook in oil 5 minutes, stirring constantly.
5. Push meat up side of wok; add radishes and scallions and cook 3 minutes, stirring constantly.
6. Stir in soup; heat, stirring occasionally.
7. Serve immediately over rice.

NOTE: Use 10-inch skillet in lieu of electric wok. After steak is cooked, push meat to the side. Add radishes and scallions and proceed as above.

Meatball Chop Suey

Serves 6 to 8

2 pounds ground beef
½ cup bread crumbs
1 cup milk
⅔ cup onion, chopped
1 egg
1 teaspoon salt
⅛ teaspoon pepper
3 tablespoons lard or drippings
2 beef bouillon cubes
3 cups hot water

¼ cup soy sauce
2 cups celery, cut into 1½-inch
   long strips
3 tablespoons cornstarch
2 tablespoons cold water
2 cans (16 ounces each) bean
   sprouts, drained
1 can (4 ounces) mushroom stems
   and pieces, drained
cooked rice and/or chow mein noodles

1. Mix ground beef, bread crumbs, milk, 2 tablespoons onion, egg, salt and pepper.
2. Shape into 24 meatballs; brown in lard or drippings. Pour off drippings.
3. Dissolve bouillon cubes in hot water; add bouillon, remaining onion, soy sauce and celery to meatballs. Cover tightly and cook slowly 15 minutes.
4. Remove meatballs.
5. Dissolve cornstarch in 2 tablespoons cold water; thicken cooking liquid with cornstarch mixture.
6. Return meatballs to sauce; add bean sprouts and mushrooms and heat.
7. Serve over cooked rice and/or chow mein noodles.

Imperial Beef

Serves 4

¼ cup slivered almonds
1 tablespoon butter or margarine
1 pound lean ground beef
1 cup water
¼ teaspoon salt

1 cup fine noodles
1 package (10 ounces) frozen
  Japanese-style vegetables
1 tablespoon soy sauce
hot cooked rice (optional)

1. Sauté almonds in butter in skillet until lightly browned; remove almonds from pan with slotted spoon and set aside.
2. Brown ground beef well in remaining butter in skillet; stir in water and salt and bring to a boil.
3. Stir in noodles; cover and simmer 2 minutes.
4. Add vegetables; bring to a full boil over medium heat, separating vegetables with fork and stirring frequently.
5. Add half the sautéed almonds; cover and simmer for 3 minutes.
6. Stir in soy sauce; sprinkle with remaining almonds.
7. Serve over hot cooked rice, if desired.

Mandarin Beef with Almond Rice

Serves 6 to 8

2 pounds stewing beef, cut in
  1½-inch cubes
2 tablespoons salad oil
½ teaspoon salt
1 teaspoon ground ginger
1 tablespoon soy sauce
1 clove garlic, minced
water

1 large green pepper, cut into
  1-inch pieces
1 large stalk celery, sliced
1 can (11 ounces) mandarin orange
  sections
1 teaspoon sugar
4 teaspoons cornstarch
Almond Rice

1. Brown beef cubes in oil; pour off drippings.
2. Combine salt, ginger, soy sauce, garlic and ½ cup water; add to beef. Cover tightly and cook slowly 1 to 1½ hours, or until tender.
3. Cook green pepper and celery in boiling water to cover 4 to 5 minutes; drain and reserve liquid.
4. Measure cooking liquid from beef; add reserved liquid from vegetables to make 1 cup.
5. Drain oranges, reserving syrup.
6. Mix together sugar, cornstarch and orange syrup; add to beef mixture and cook, stirring constantly, until thickened.
7. Add green pepper, celery and orange sections; heat. Serve with Almond Rice.

Almond Rice

¼ cup slivered almonds
2 tablespoons butter or margarine

2 cups cooked instant rice (prepared
  according to package directions)

1. Brown almonds in butter.
2. Add almonds to hot cooked rice; toss lightly before serving.

Emir's Beef Curry

Serves 4 to 6

2 tablespoons butter or margarine
2 teaspoons curry powder
1 teaspoon instant onion flakes
2 tablespoons flour
¼ teaspoon salt
¼ teaspoon white pepper
1¼ cups milk
fresh lemon juice

1½ to 2 cups cooked beef, chicken
  or pork, cubed
hot cooked rice
2 hard-cooked eggs (for garnish)
curry condiments: chopped peanuts,
  minced onion, coconut, raisins,
  crisp bacon and chutney

1. Melt butter and stir in curry powder; cook over low heat 2 to 3 minutes.
2. Add onion, flour, salt and white pepper; mix until blended and smooth. Cook and stir until bubbly.
3. Remove from heat and stir in milk; return to heat and cook, stirring until thickened.
4. Add lemon juice to taste and cubed beef; simmer until heated through.
5. Serve hot over rice; garnish with quartered hard-cooked eggs.
6. Provide condiments such as chopped peanuts, minced onion, coconut, raisins, crumbled crisp bacon, chutney and others.

Junk Meatballs Cantonese

Serves 6

1 pound lean ground beef
¾ cup celery, minced
¼ cup almonds, finely chopped
1½ teaspoons seasoned salt
½ cup dry bread crumbs
4 tablespoons teriyaki barbecue
  marinade

2 eggs, slightly beaten
cornstarch
3 tablespoons corn oil
1 can (13¼ ounces) pineapple chunks
water
1 green bell pepper, cut into slivers
fluffy rice

1. Combine ground beef, celery, almonds, seasoned salt, bread crumbs, 1 tablespoon teriyaki barbecue marinade and eggs; shape into balls about 1½ inches in diameter. (Mixture will make about 18 meatballs.)
2. Roll balls in cornstarch; brown in hot oil.
3. Reduce heat; simmer about 15 minutes, turning frequently. Drain fat.
4. Combine 3 tablespoons cornstarch and remaining 3 tablespoons teriyaki barbecue marinade.
5. Drain liquid from pineapple and add enough water to make 2 cups; blend with cornstarch and pour over meatballs.
6. Add pineapple chunks and green pepper; cook, stirring constantly, until thickened and pineapple and pepper are heated through.
7. Serve over fluffy rice.

Plum Wonderful Steak Kabobs

Serves 4

1 pound flank steak
1 teaspoon pepper
2 cans (1 pound each) purple plums
   in water
4 teaspoons fresh lime juice

2 tablespoons soy sauce
2 containers (8 ounces each)
   plain yogurt
2 limes
watercress (for garnish)

1. Pound steak with meat mallet, keeping steak whole. Rub with pepper, then cut in half lengthwise.
2. Drain plums; combine ½ cup liquid with lime juice, soy sauce and ½ cup yogurt.
3. Spread both sides of steak with some of marinade mixture; roll tightly with the grain and fasten with skewers about 1 inch apart.
4. Cut between skewers to make slices about 1 inch thick.
5. Coat plums with remaining marinade; alternate plums and steak rolls on skewers.
6. Broil about 15 minutes, turning once.
7. Cut limes in halves and add to skewers.
8. Serve remaining yogurt in bowl surrounded with garnish of watercress.

NOTE: Great for dieters – 336 calories per serving!

Steak-on-a-Stake

Serves 6

1½ pounds boneless beef loin
   sirloin steak, cut ¾ inch thick
½ cup soy sauce
2 tablespoons honey
½ teaspoon ground ginger
1 clove garlic, crushed

2 teaspoons sesame oil or salad oil
2 tablespoons dry sherry
pineapple chunks, fresh or canned
   (for garnish)
1 green pepper, cut into strips
   (for garnish)

1. Cut meat into strips about ¾ inch wide and 2 inches long; place in shallow baking dish.
2. Mix remaining ingredients except pineapple and green pepper; cover and refrigerate 1 to 2 hours, turning once.
3. Remove beef strips from marinade, reserving marinade; thread on 9- to 10-inch bamboo skewers, using about 5 pieces of meat.
4. Grill 4 inches from medium-hot coals until meat is browned, 4 to 5 minutes on each side, basting with marinade, if desired.
5. Garnish with pineapple chunks and green pepper strips.

NOTE: Good for outdoor cooking or patio supper!

Curried Lamb with Bananas

Serves 4 to 6

4 lamb shanks
3 cups water
1 teaspoon salt
1 small bay leaf
½ cup onion, finely chopped

¼ cup butter
1 teaspoon curry powder
⅓ cup flour
½ cup raisins
2 bananas
hot cooked rice

1. Simmer lamb shanks with water, salt and bay leaf in a covered pan until tender, about 1 hour.
2. Lift out lamb and remove meat from bones; cut into bite-size pieces and set aside.
3. Measure lamb broth; add water to make 3 cups.
4. Cook onions in melted butter in large skillet until tender but not browned; stir in curry powder, then flour. Cook 1 minute.
5. Add broth; cook and stir until thickened. Add meat and raisins.
6. Just before serving, slice bananas diagonally; add to meat and heat.
7. Serve over hot cooked rice.

Gingered Lamb & Vegetables Orientale

Serves 2 to 4

1 pound lean lamb, cut into
  thin strips
2 tablespoons corn oil
1 cup scallions, sliced lengthwise
1 can (4 ounces) whole mushrooms
1 can (5 ounces) bamboo shoots,
  drained

½ cup water chestnuts, sliced
3 tablespoons soy sauce
1 tablespoon ginger root, shredded, or
  1 teaspoon ground ginger
1 tablespoon cornstarch
cold water
cooked rice or Chinese noodles

1. Quickly brown lamb in hot oil in wok or skillet, stirring constantly.
2. Remove lamb; set aside.
3. Add scallions; cook until brown.
4. Drain mushrooms, reserving liquid.
5. Add mushrooms, lamb, bamboo shoots, water chestnuts, soy sauce and ginger to scallions in skillet; heat through, stirring constantly.
6. Dissolve cornstarch in ¼ cup cold water; add mushroom liquid and enough water to measure 1 cup.
7. Blend cornstarch-mushroom liquid into lamb mixture; cover and cook over medium heat, stirring constantly, until thickened and clear.
8. Serve with cooked rice or Chinese noodles.

NOTE: For flavorful additions or substitutions, add diagonally sliced carrots and celery, snow pea pods, zucchini, broccoli, asparagus, Chinese cabbage, green beans, green peppers and quartered tomatoes. Dieter's delight, at approximately 200 calories per serving!

Limed Lamb Shreds with Leeks

Serves 4

1½ pounds boneless lamb,
  partially frozen
4 tablespoons soy sauce
¼ cup plus 1 tablespoon water
1 tablespoon sherry

1 teaspoon ginger root, slivered
¼ teaspoon crushed red pepper
2 teaspoons fresh lime juice
8 trimmed leeks (white part only),
  sliced diagonally

2 teaspoons grated lime rind

1. Carve partially frozen lamb against grain into thin slices; cut each slice into 2 to 3 long strips.
2. Arrange strips on rack in a pan; roast at 350° F. 5 to 8 minutes, or until meat is rare.
3. Combine soy sauce, 1 tablespoon water, sherry, ginger and red pepper; pour mixture over lamb and marinate 20 minutes.
4. Bring remaining water and lime juice to a boil in wok or skillet.
5. Drain lamb mixture and discard liquid; add lamb to wok and cook, stirring, 2 minutes, or until lamb loses pink color.
6. Add leeks; continue to cook, stirring, about 1 minute.
7. Stir in lime rind; toss and cook 1 to 2 minutes longer to combine flavors.

Yushan-Style Spring Lamb

Serves 4

¼ cup soy sauce
1 teaspoon dry sherry
½ teaspoon ground ginger
1 pound uncooked New Zealand
  spring lamb (leg or shoulder),
  cut in strips
3 tablespoons corn oil
1 large onion, peeled and sliced

1 green pepper, cut in cubes
1 clove garlic, minced
2 tablespoons cornstarch
¼ cup water
1 can (8 ounces) water chestnuts,
  drained and thinly sliced
1 package (6 ounces) frozen pea pods
⅛ teaspoon Tabasco sauce

hot cooked rice

1. Combine soy sauce, sherry and ginger in medium bowl; add meat and marinate, covered, in refrigerator at least 2 hours.
2. Remove meat from marinade; reserve marinade.
3. Heat 1 tablespoon oil in large skillet over medium-high heat; stir-fry lamb 3 minutes.
4. Remove meat to small bowl.
5. In same skillet, heat remaining 2 tablespoons oil; sauté onion, green pepper and garlic 2 minutes.
6. Dissolve cornstarch in water; add to reserved marinade.
7. Return meat to skillet; add water chestnuts and marinade. Cook over low heat, stirring constantly, until sauce boils and thickens.
8. Add pea pods and Tabasco sauce; heat through.
9. Serve with hot cooked rice.

Banana Sweet & Sour Pork

Serves 4

2 tablespoons corn or peanut oil
1½ pounds pork shoulder, cut
   into ½-inch cubes
1 can (15¼ ounces) pineapple
   tidbits in syrup
water
½ cup white vinegar
1 tablespoon catsup

½ teaspoon original Worcestershire sauce
¼ cup packed brown sugar
½ teaspoon salt
½ cup celery, sliced
2 scallions, sliced
1 green pepper, cut in strips
1 tablespoon cornstarch

2 bananas, sliced

1. Heat oil in large skillet; add pork and brown lightly.
2. Drain syrup from pineapple into measuring cup; add enough water to make 1 cup.
3. Add pineapple syrup and water, vinegar, catsup, Worcestershire sauce, brown sugar and salt to skillet; cover and simmer 45 minutes, until pork is tender.
4. Add celery, scallions and green pepper; cook 10 minutes.
5. Dissolve cornstarch in ¼ cup water; stir into pork mixture. Simmer 2 to 3 minutes, until slightly thickened.
6. Peel bananas and cut into slices; add to pork along with pineapple. Serve immediately.

Cantonese Pork Steak Strips

Serves 6

3 pork blade steaks, cut ¾-inch
   thick (about 2 pounds)
1 tablespoon corn oil
1 teaspoon salt
½ teaspoon ground ginger
2 cups water
carrots, peeled and cut in 2-inch
   strips
2 cups celery, cut in 1-inch pieces
1 large onion, peeled and cut in
   8 wedges

¼ cup soy sauce
1 tablespoon brown sugar or honey
1 tablespoon fresh lemon juice
1 can (4 ounces) mushroom stems
   and pieces
¼ cup cornstarch
1 can (16 ounces) bean sprouts,
   drained
chow mein noodles or rice

1. Cut pork steak into 2 x ¼-inch strips; brown in corn oil in frying pan. Pour off drippings.
2. Sprinkle meat with salt and ginger; stir in water.
3. Add carrots, celery, onions, soy sauce, brown sugar and lemon juice; cook slowly, covered, 40 minutes, or until meat is tender, stirring occasionally.
4. Drain mushrooms, reserving liquid; blend liquid with cornstarch and stir into meat mixture.
5. Add mushrooms and bean sprouts; cook, stirring constantly, until mixture thickens.
6. Serve with chow mein noodles or rice.

Chinese Pork Shoulder Steaks

Serves 4 to 6

1 beef bouillon cube
⅓ cup hot water
1 teaspoon ground ginger
2 teaspoons salt
1 tablespoon sugar

¼ cup honey
¼ cup soy sauce
4 to 6 pork arm or blade steaks,
cut ¾ inch thick

1. Dissolve bouillon cube in hot water.
2. Combine ginger, salt, sugar, honey and soy sauce; add to bouillon.
3. Marinate steaks in soy sauce mixture in refrigerator for 2 hours, turning occasionally.
4. Remove steaks from marinade; place on grill over glowing coals 3 inches from heat.
5. Grill 30 to 45 minutes, brushing frequently with marinade.
6. Turn after grilling 15 minutes; continue cooking until done.

Far-Eastern Butterfly Pork Chops

Serves 6

6 butterfly pork chops,
cut ¾ to 1 inch thick
2 tablespoons lard or drippings
½ teaspoon salt
¼ cup soy sauce
3 tablespoons honey
1 clove garlic, peeled and minced
½ teaspoon ginger
½ cup boiling water
2 cups celery, sliced
1 large green pepper, cut in strips

2 tablespoons cornstarch
¼ cup cold water
6 to 8 scallions, cut in 1½-inch
pieces
1 can (6 ounces) water chestnuts,
drained and halved
1 jar (4 ounces) pimiento, cut in
½-inch-wide strips
1 package (6 ounces) frozen
Chinese pea pods

1. Brown chops in lard in heavy frying pan; pour off drippings.
2. Salt chops on both sides; cover tightly and cook slowly, 30 minutes.
3. Combine soy sauce, honey, garlic and ginger; bring to a boil.
4. Pour sauce over chops and cook slowly, covered, 15 to 30 minutes, or until chops are tender.
5. Pour boiling water over celery and green pepper in saucepan; cook, covered, 2 to 3 minutes until vegetables are tender-crisp. Drain, reserving liquid.
6. Remove chops to heated platter; add reserved vegetable liquid to soy-honey liquid in frying pan to make 1 cup.
7. Combine cornstarch and cold water; add to same pan. Cook, stirring, until sauce thickens.
8. Stir in celery, green pepper, scallions, water chestnuts, pimiento and pea pods, separating the pods; cook slowly until vegetables are heated through, 2 to 3 minutes.

Chow Mein Noodle-Pork Vegetable Medley

Serves 4

¾ pound lean boneless pork or chicken, cut in thin strips
1 tablespoon sherry
2 tablespoons soy sauce
2 tablespoons cornstarch
1 teaspoon salt
1 teaspoon sugar
pepper to taste
1 package (6.35 ounces) chow mein noodles
2 quarts boiling water

6½ tablespoons salad oil
1 small onion, peeled and chopped
2 stalks celery, chopped
½ green pepper, thinly sliced
2 scallions, chopped
½ pound mushrooms, sliced
2 ounces snow peas
½ pound bean sprouts
⅔ cup chicken broth
2 tablespoons cold water

1. Marinate pork in mixture of 1 tablespoon each sherry, soy sauce and cornstarch; and ½ teaspoon each salt and sugar and pepper to taste.
2. Cook chow mein noodles in 2 quarts boiling water, stirring constantly for 2 minutes. Rinse twice with cold water and drain well. Toss lightly with ½ tablespoon oil.
3. Heat 3 tablespoons oil in wok or large skillet to smoking point; arrange noodles in wok and cook over moderate heat until golden brown and crisp (forms large pancake). Turn over carefully; brown other side. (If noodles stick, add small amount of oil around edge of wok or pan.)
4. When crisp on both sides, place noodle pancake on platter; keep warm.
5. Heat 1 tablespoon oil in wok. Add onion, celery and green pepper; stir-fry 1 minute. Remove to bowl.
6. Add 1 tablespoon oil to wok and heat; add scallions and mushrooms; stir-fry quickly.
7. Add snow peas and bean sprouts; stir-fry until slightly wilted. Remove to large bowl.
8. Add 1 tablespoon oil to wok; stir-fry half the meat until it loses its red color. Remove to bowl.
9. Repeat with remaining meat.
10. Return all meat and vegetables to wok; quickly add remaining ½ teaspoon salt, ½ teaspoon sugar and 1 tablespoon soy sauce. Add chicken broth.
11. Stir remaining 1 tablespoon cornstarch into 2 tablespoons cold water; add slowly to thicken sauce. Cook and stir until sauce is clear.
12. Serve over bed of warm chow mein noodles (pancake).

NOTE: *Deliciously different! Excellent example of a meal-in-one, made with Japanese wheat flour noodles.*

Braised Ginger Pork

Serves 6

2 pounds lean 1-inch pork cubes
flour
3 tablespoons peanut oil
⅓ cup chicken broth
⅓ cup soy sauce
2 tablespoons sherry

¼ cup scallions, chopped
1 small clove garlic, crushed
1 tablespoon sugar
1 teaspoon ground ginger
dash freshly ground black pepper
hot cooked rice

1. Dredge meat in flour; set on plate.
2. Heat oil in Dutch oven or large skillet; add half the meat and brown quickly; remove meat and set aside.
3. Brown remaining meat; remove and set aside.
4. Pour off excess oil.
5. Return meat to pan with chicken broth, soy sauce and sherry; add scallions, garlic, sugar, ginger and pepper. Simmer, covered, for 15 minutes, or until meat is tender.
6. Serve over hot cooked rice.

Hunan Pork

Serves 6

1 egg, slightly beaten
½ cup cornstarch
¼ cup unsifted flour
¾ teaspoon salt
2¾ cups chicken broth or
   bouillon
¼ cup sesame or salad oil
6 pork chops, about 1 inch thick,
   trimmed of fat
1 pound carrots, peeled and cut into
   thin 3-inch-long strips

½ cup sugar
½ cup red wine vinegar
¼ cup sweet pickle liquid
2 teaspoons soy sauce
½ cup water
1 bunch scallions, cut into 2-inch
   pieces (about 1½ cups)
1 cup sweet mixed pickles, drained
4 cups hot cooked rice

1. Mix together egg, ¼ cup cornstarch, flour, salt and ¼ cup chicken broth.
2. Heat oil in large skillet; dip pork chops into batter; fry in hot oil until lightly browned on both sides.
3. Transfer browned chops to rack in shallow baking pan; bake, uncovered, in preheated 375° F. oven for 35 minutes.
4. Meanwhile, discard all but 2 tablespoons oil in skillet; sauté carrots in oil until crisp-tender, about 10 minutes.
5. Add sugar, vinegar, pickle liquid, soy sauce and remaining chicken broth.
6. Combine remaining ¼ cup cornstarch with water and gradually stir into broth mixture; stir constantly until mixture thickens. Simmer about 3 minutes.
7. Add scallions and pickles; simmer about 2 minutes more.
8. Arrange pork chops on bed of rice and pour some of sauce over chops; serve remaining sauce in small bowl.

Orange Sausage Bundles

Serves 4

1 package (¾ pound) smoked
    sausage links
1 can (1 pound) sweet potatoes,
    drained and sliced

1 large orange, cut in 8 slices
½ cup orange marmalade
¼ cup almonds, slivered

1. For each bundle, arrange 2 smoked sausages, several slices sweet potato and 2 orange slices on large piece of heavy-duty foil.
2. Spread 2 tablespoons orange marmalade over bundle; sprinkle with 1 tablespoon almonds. Repeat with remaining bundles.
3. Fold edges of foil to seal securely. Place on outdoor grill; heat bundles through, at least 15 minutes.

Pork Sate with Peanut Sauce

Serves 4

2 tablespoons peanut oil
1 tablespoon curry powder
¼ cup soy sauce
¼ cup creamy peanut butter
¼ cup peanuts, finely chopped
1 tablespoon firmly-packed light
    brown sugar

2 tablespoons fresh lime juice
½ teaspoon crushed red pepper
1 clove garlic, crushed
1 pound boneless pork loin, cut in
    1-inch cubes
3 cups hot cooked rice
Peanut Sauce

1. Mix peanut oil and curry powder in small saucepan; simmer over low heat 2 minutes.
2. Gradually blend soy sauce into creamy peanut butter in bowl; stir in peanuts, curry mixture, sugar, lime juice, red pepper and garlic.
3. Add pork cubes, tossing well to coat all sides.
4. Cover bowl tightly; chill 4 hours, or overnight.
5. Thread marinated pork cubes onto skewers; broil slowly, about 6 inches from heat, or grill over barbecue, turning often, until pork is tender and cooked, about 20 to 25 minutes.
6. Serve with hot cooked rice and Peanut Sauce.

Peanut Sauce

2 tablespoons peanut oil
¼ cup scallions, chopped
½ cup peanuts, ground
2 cups chicken broth
1 tablespoon light brown sugar

1 teaspoon fresh lime juice
¼ teaspoon ground ginger
⅛ teaspoon chili powder
1 tablespoon water
1 tablespoon cornstarch

1. Heat peanut oil in saucepan; add scallions and sauté just until tender.
2. Stir in peanuts, chicken broth, sugar, lime juice, ginger and chili powder; cook over medium-high heat, stirring constantly, until mixture comes to a boil.
3. Reduce heat and simmer, uncovered, for 15 minutes.
4. Mix water and cornstarch; blend into hot sauce and cook, stirring, until thickened.
5. Keep sauce warm until ready to serve.

Pork Chop Suey

Serves 6

2 cups cooked pork, diced
¼ cup mushrooms, sliced
2 tablespoons corn oil
1 cup celery, thinly sliced
1 small carrot, cut in thin strips
1 medium onion, sliced
1½ cups beef broth

2 cups canned bean sprouts,
  with liquid
3 tablespoons cornstarch
3 tablespoons soy sauce
salt to taste
pepper to taste
1½ cups hot cooked rice

1. Cook pork and mushrooms in hot oil over low heat a few minutes, until lightly browned.
2. Add celery, carrot, onion, and broth; cover pan and cook gently 10 to 15 minutes, or until vegetables are tender.
3. Add bean sprouts and liquid; heat to boiling.
4. Mix cornstarch and soy sauce, add gradually to boiling mixture, stirring constantly. Cook 2 minutes, or until slightly thickened.
5. Add salt and pepper to taste; serve over rice.

Imperial Pork Loin

Serves 6 to 8

6 pounds center-cut pork loin roast
1 can (1 pound 4 ounces) sliced
  pineapple
½ cup naturally brewed soy sauce

½ cup apricot-pineapple jam
2 tablespoons crystallized ginger,
  minced
1 tablespoon cornstarch

1. Have butcher loosen backbone of roast. Place roast, fat-side up, on rack in open roasting pan; insert meat thermometer with bulb in thickest part, not touching bone.
2. Roast in preheated 325° F. oven 2½ hours, or until thermometer registers 170° F.
3. Meanwhile, drain pineapple well, reserving all syrup; blend syrup with soy sauce, jam and ginger and pour over pineapple to marinate.
4. Brush pork with marinade every 10 minutes during last ½ hour of cooking.
5. Pour remaining marinade into saucepan; blend in cornstarch and cook, stirring constantly, until sauce thickens.
6. Cut pork into serving portions; serve with pineapple and sauce.

Pork Chow Mein

Serves 6

1½ pounds pork, cut in ¾-inch
  pieces
2 tablespoons salad oil
½ teaspoon salt
1 large onion, cut in 8 wedges
½ cup water
1 small head cabbage, shredded
  (8 cups)

1 can (16 ounces) bean sprouts,
  drained
⅓ cup soy sauce
2 tablespoons cornstarch
⅛ teaspoon ginger
chow mein noodles

1. Brown pork in oil in large frying pan.
2. Sprinkle with salt; add onions and water. Cover tightly and cook slowly 45 minutes.
3. Add cabbage and cook 10 minutes; stir in bean sprouts.
4. Blend soy sauce with cornstarch and ginger; gradually add to pork mixture, stirring to blend.
5. Cook until thickened, stirring occasionally.
6. Serve on chow mein noodles.

Stir-Fry Pork with Almonds

Serves 4

1 pound lean pork loin or rump,
  cut into thin strips
¼ cup soy sauce
2 tablespoons vinegar
1 tablespoon brown sugar
½ cup dry sherry
½ teaspoon dry mustard
½ teaspoon ground ginger
⅛ teaspoon garlic powder

1 tablespoon cornstarch
¼ cup peanut or vegetable oil
½ cup whole blanched almonds
2 onions, peeled and cut into
  narrow wedges
½ pound fresh green beans,
  trimmed and halved, or 1 package
  (9 ounces) frozen cut, whole or
  French-cut green beans, thawed
  and drained

1. Combine pork, soy sauce, vinegar, sugar, sherry, mustard, ginger, garlic powder and cornstarch; marinate at least 15 minutes.
2. Heat oil in wok or skillet; add almonds and roast until golden brown. Lift out and set aside.
3. Lift pork from marinade with slotted spoon; add to hot skillet and cook until browned, stirring just a little, about 2 minutes.
4. Add onions and beans; reduce heat to medium-high, cover, and cook, shaking pan often for even cooking, 5 minutes, or until tender-crisp.
5. Stir in almonds and remaining marinade; cook, stirring, 1 minute, or just until hot and glazed.

Pork Lo Mein

Serves 6

1 package (8 ounces) vermicelli
6 pork chops (about 3½ pounds)
¼ cup corn oil
2 cups onions, sliced
2 cloves garlic, minced
1 can (16 ounces) Chinese vegetables

2 to 3 canned water chestnuts, sliced
1 package (6 ounces) Chinese pea pods
2 tablespoons cornstarch
2 teaspoons ground ginger
1 can (13½ ounces) chicken broth
½ cup soy sauce

finely sliced scallions and pimientos (optional garnish)

1. Cook vermicelli according to package directions; drain and set aside.
2. Trim pork from bone; trim meat and discard fat. Cut meat into paper-thin strips.
3. Heat oil in wok or large skillet; stir-fry meat at high heat until brown.
4. Reduce heat and add onions and garlic; cook until vegetables are soft and tender.
5. Rinse Chinese vegetables under cold running water; drain well.
6. Add vegetables to wok, along with cooked vermicelli, water chestnuts and pea pods.
7. In a small bowl, blend cornstarch and ginger slowly with chicken broth until smooth; add soy sauce. Pour into skillet and stir until sauce boils and thickens.
8. Serve at once, garnished with scallions and pimientos, if desired.

Sweet & Sour Spareribs

Serves 4

3 pounds spareribs cut in serving-size pieces
⅔ cup dark brown sugar, packed
2 tablespoons cornstarch
2 teaspoons dry mustard
⅔ cup vinegar
1 can (8¼ ounces) crushed pineapple, undrained

½ cup catsup
½ cup water
1 small yellow onion, peeled and chopped
2 tablespoons soy sauce
salt to taste
pepper to taste

1. Spread ribs, fatty-side down, in single layer in large shallow pan; brown in 425° F. oven 20 to 30 minutes. Drain off fat.
2. In a saucepan, combine remaining ingredients except salt and pepper; stir until smooth.
3. Cook sauce over medium heat until thick and glossy, stirring constantly.
4. Sprinkle salt and pepper over browned ribs; spoon sweet-sour sauce over each piece, using half the sauce.
5. Reduce oven temperature to 350° F.; bake 45 minutes longer.
6. Turn ribs and cover with remaining sauce; bake 30 minutes more, or until well done.

Fukien Pork & Tomatoes

Serves 4 to 6

3 tablespoons cornstarch
3 tablespoons naturally brewed soy sauce
1 teaspoon sugar
1 teaspoon fresh ginger root, minced
1 clove garlic, crushed

¾ pound boneless pork, sliced in thin strips
1 cup water
2 tablespoons corn or peanut oil
1 medium green pepper, chunked

3 tomatoes, cut in eighths

1. Blend together in bowl 1 tablespoon each cornstarch and soy sauce; add sugar, ginger and garlic.
2. Add pork, stirring until pieces are well coated; marinate 15 minutes.
3. Meanwhile, combine water with remaining cornstarch and soy sauce; set aside.
4. Heat oil in large frying pan or wok over high heat; add pork and stir-fry until golden brown.
5. Cover, reduce heat, and simmer 15 minutes.
6. Add green pepper; stir-fry until tender-crisp.
7. Stir in tomatoes and soy sauce mixture and bring to a boil; cook only until sauce thickens. Serve immediately.

Tim Suen Yoke
(Sweet & Sour Pork)

Serves 4

1 pound boneless lean pork
2 eggs
½ teaspoon salt
½ cup flour
corn or peanut oil

1 cup pineapple chunks, drained
6 small sweet pickles, sliced
1 green pepper, cut in squares
3 small carrots, sliced
½ cup water

1. Cut pork into 1-inch cubes.
2. Beat eggs slightly and mix with flour and salt to make a batter.
3. Dip pork into batter and fry in deep hot oil for 10 minutes.
4. Remove meat and drain on paper towels.
5. Place pork in a dry skillet with pineapple, pickles, green pepper and carrots; add water, cover, and cook for 10 minutes.

For the Sauce

3 tablespoons vinegar
2 teaspoons sugar
1 tablespoon cornstarch

1 tablespoon molasses
1 cup water
1 tablespoon Angostura bitters

1. Blend all ingredients; add to meat mixture, stirring gently but thoroughly.
2. Heat 5 minutes; serve immediately.

Pineapple-Marinated Spareribs

Serves 6 to 8

¾ cup pineapple preserves
½ cup fresh orange juice
1 tablespoon fresh lime or lemon
  juice
⅓ cup soy sauce
1 teaspoon ground ginger

¼ teaspoon rosemary
¼ teaspoon ground black pepper
1 clove garlic, peeled and minced
4 to 6 pounds spareribs, cut into
  serving-size pieces

1. Mix together all ingredients except spareribs.
2. Put spareribs in shallow dish; pour marinade over ribs and marinate in refrigerator 3 to 4 hours, or longer, turning 2 or 3 times.
3. Remove spareribs; place on rack in open roasting pan. (Do not add water or cover.) Roast in preheated 350° F. oven 2 to 2½ hours, basting with marinade every 30 minutes.

Spareribs Orientale

Serves 4 to 6

4 pounds spareribs, cut into
  2-rib sections
2 to 4 fresh nectarines
2 tablespoons cornstarch
½ cup water
1 teaspoon salt

½ cup brown sugar, packed
½ cup lemon juice
¼ cup vinegar
1 tablespoon soy sauce
½ cup green pepper, sliced
1 cup onions, thinly sliced

1. Place ribs in 13 x 9-inch baking dish; bake at 350° F. for 1½ hours. Drain off fat.
2. Meanwhile, slice nectarines to yield 2 cups; set aside.
3. Blend cornstarch with water in saucepan; add all remaining ingredients and cook, stirring, until sauce is thickened and clear.
4. Add nectarines; pour sauce over spareribs and bake 30 minutes longer, or until ribs are done.

Jou Ssu Pai Ts' Ai
(Cabbage & Meat Shreds)

Serves 4

¼ cup margarine
1 medium head cabbage, shredded
1 bunch scallions, sliced

1 pound lean pork, shredded
2 tablespoons soy sauce
1 tablespoon sherry

1 teaspoon sugar

1. Melt 1 tablespoon margarine in skillet or wok; add cabbage and sauté, tossing constantly, for 5 minutes. Remove cabbage from skillet.
2. Melt remaining margarine in same skillet; add scallions and pork shreds. Cook 3 to 5 minutes, stirring constantly, or until pink of meat has disappeared.
3. Stir in soy sauce, sherry, sugar and cabbage; cook 2 minutes more.

Heavenly Pork with Choy Sum

Serves 4

1½ pounds boneless pork,
 partially frozen
2 tablespoons sherry
½ teaspoon lemon-pepper seasoning
2 teaspoons cornstarch

2 cups sliced choy sum (Chinese greens)
2 tablespoons soy sauce
1 teaspoon chili sauce
1 teaspoon garlic, minced
1 teaspoon ginger root, grated

1 Cut pork against the grain into thin slices; arrange slices on rack in pan and roast in preheated 350° F. oven 8 to 10 minutes, or until pork loses pink color.
2. Combine sherry and lemon-pepper; sprinkle evenly over pork. Set aside for 10 minutes.
3. Sprinkle pork slices evenly with cornstarch; roast at 500° F. 15 to 20 minutes, or until pork is sizzling and browned.
4. Place choy sum in wok; stir-fry over high heat 2 minutes, or until wilted.
5. Combine soy, chili sauce, garlic and ginger; stir soy mixture into greens.
6. Add pork; cover, reduce heat, and cook 2 minutes.

Cantonese Pork Dinner

Serves 6 to 8

2 pounds boneless pork shoulder,
 sliced in thin strips
2 tablespoons lard or drippings
1 package (1¼ ounces) onion
 soup mix
1¾ cups water
2 tablespoons soy sauce

2 tablespoons cornstarch
1 cup fresh mushrooms, sliced
 lengthwise
1 can (6 ounces) water chestnuts,
 drained and sliced
1 package (9 ounces) frozen
 Italian green beans
hot cooked rice

1. Cut each pork cube in slices ¼- to ⅓-inch thick; brown in lard or drippings.
2. Combine soup mix with 1½ cups water and soy sauce; add to pork. Cover tightly and cook slowly 30 to 40 minutes, or until meat is tender.
3. Blend ¼ cup water with cornstarch; add to meat mixture. Cook, stirring constantly, until thickened.
4. Add mushrooms, water chestnuts and Italian green beans (separated but not defrosted); continue cooking slowly, covered, 7 minutes, or until meat and vegetables are done.
5. Serve with hot cooked rice.

Browned Rice with Cashews

Serves 4

non-stick cooking spray
⅔ cup rice
2 tablespoons chopped scallions

2 tablespoons chopped cashews
1½ cups water
½ teaspoon salt

few grains pepper

1. Coat inside of medium saucepan with cooking spray according to directions; heat over medium heat.
2. Add rice, scallions, and cashews; cook and stir until rice is lightly browned.
3. Stir in water, salt and pepper; bring to a boil.
4. Cover and simmer over low heat 15 minutes, or until rice is tender.

Na Meshi
(Green Rice)

Serves 4 to 6

1 pound fresh spinach or broccoli
water

sea salt to taste (about 1½ teaspoons)
4 cups hot cooked rice

1. Wash spinach or broccoli carefully. (If using broccoli, chop into bite-size pieces.)
2. Place in saucepan with small amount of water; steam a few minutes (only until spinach or broccoli is crisp-tender).
3. Press in colander to remove excess water; sprinkle with sea salt to taste.
4. Toss lightly with hot cooked rice; serve at once.

Currant Rice

Serves 8 to 10

½ cup currants
¼ cup white wine
2 tablespoons butter
½ cup vermicelli, broken in
    ½-inch pieces
1 cup medium- or long-grain rice
1½ cups onions, chopped

1 can (10½ ounces) condensed
    chicken broth
1 soup can water
½ teaspoon dry mustard
dash cayenne
1 tablespoon soy sauce
½ cup yogurt

1. In small saucepan, combine currants and wine; bring to a boil, cover, and simmer for 1 minute.
2. Remove from heat and set aside.
3. In 2-quart saucepan, melt butter; add vermicelli and sauté until browned.
4. Add remaining ingredients except yogurt; bring to a boil, cover, and simmer 12 to 15 minutes, or until rice is tender.
5. Stir in currants and yogurt; heat for a minute, then serve.

NOTE: Mixture is moist and may be prepared in advance and reheated.

Apricot-Ginger Oriental Rice

Serves 6

3 tablespoons butter or margarine
1 cup rice
½ cup onion, chopped
¼ teaspoon ground ginger
2 cups chicken broth

1 cup dried apricots, diced
⅓ cup raisins
½ cup celery, chopped
½ cup peanuts
salt to taste

1. Melt butter in large skillet; add rice and onion and cook until golden.
2. Add ginger, chicken broth, apricots and raisins; simmer, covered, about 10 minutes, or until rice is almost tender.
3. Stir in celery; cook until rice is tender.
4. Mix peanuts into rice and season to taste with salt.

Fried Bacon Rice

Serves 6

6 slices bacon, diced
2 eggs, slightly beaten
6 cups cold cooked rice

8 medium scallions, sliced
¼ cup naturally brewed soy sauce
1 teaspoon sugar

¼ teaspoon ground white pepper

1. Fry bacon until crisp; remove all but 3 tablespoons drippings from pan.
2. Push bacon to one side; add eggs to pan and scramble.
3. Stir in rice, scallions, soy sauce, sugar and pepper; heat through, stirring occasionally.

Ham Fried Rice

Serves 6

¼ cup corn oil
2 cloves garlic, minced
4 cups boiled rice, at least
  1 day old
½ cup cooked ham or pork, diced

¼ cup soy sauce
2 tablespoons dry sherry
¾ teaspoon ground ginger
½ teaspoon Tabasco pepper sauce
2 eggs, beaten

2 tablespoons minced parsley

1. Heat oil in wok or large skillet over high heat; add garlic and sauté 1 minute.
2. Add rice; stir until grains separate and rice is hot.
3. Push rice to side of wok; add ham and stir-fry 1 minute. Stir into rice.
4. Combine soy sauce, sherry, ginger and Tabasco sauce; pour over rice, stirring to mix well.
5. Push mixture to side of wok; add eggs and stir until eggs are set. Break eggs into small pieces and stir into rice mixture.
6. Serve hot, sprinkled with parsley; if desired, serve with additional Tabasco sauce.

Peanut-Brown Rice Oriental

Serves 6

1½ cups brown rice
1 can (11 ounces) mandarin orange sections
½ cup soy sauce
3 cups water
1½ tablespoons butter or margarine
1 large clove garlic, crushed

1 cup celery, thinly sliced
½ cup scallions, sliced
1 cup salted peanuts
2 tablespoons honey
1 tablespoon fresh lemon juice
1 pound bean sprouts
3 tablespoons parsley, chopped

1. Put rice in a large skillet.
2. Drain oranges, reserving ½ cup of liquid; set oranges aside.
3. Add reserved liquid to rice in skillet; add soy sauce, water, butter and garlic; stir to combine.
4. Cover skillet and simmer mixture about 45 minutes, or until rice is tender and all the liquid has been absorbed.
5. Add celery, scallions, and peanuts during the last 5 minutes of cooking.
6. Stir in honey, lemon juice, bean sprouts, reserved oranges and parsley.

Jade Noodles

Serves 6

½ pound fresh Chinese noodles or vermicelli
boiling water
2 tablespoons sesame seed oil
¼ cup pine nuts (for garnish)
2 tablespoons vegetable oil
2 cloves garlic, peeled and minced
¼ to ½ teaspoon red pepper flakes

1 bag (10 ounces) spinach, washed, with water clinging to leaves
¼ cup chicken broth
1 teaspoon salt
1 teaspoon sugar
dash white pepper
2 teaspoons fresh lemon juice
1 teaspoon dry white wine
12 cherry tomatoes, halved

1. Cook noodles in boiling water until al dente; about 3 minutes.
2. Drain noodles and toss with sesame oil; set aside in heated serving platter or bowl.
3. Toast pine nuts in vegetable oil in wok or large skillet; remove nuts and set aside.
4. Add garlic, red pepper flakes and spinach to hot oil in same wok or skillet; cook and stir 30 seconds.
5. Stir in chicken broth, salt, sugar, pepper, lemon juice and wine; heat through, stirring and tossing ingredients all the while.
6. Stir in tomatoes.
7. Spoon hot spinach mixture over noodles; garnish with pine nuts.

Curried Eggs

Serves 4

2 cups plain yogurt
3 tablespoons all-purpose flour
¾ teaspoon curry powder
6 hard-cooked eggs
¼ cup scallions, sliced

2 tablespoons chutney (optional)
¼ teaspoon salt
dash pepper
1 package (10 ounces) chopped
  broccoli, cooked and drained

1. Blend together yogurt, flour and curry powder in medium saucepan.
2. Cut slices from center of two eggs for garnish, if desired; chop all remaining eggs and stir into yogurt mixture, along with scallions, chutney (if desired), salt and pepper.
3. Cook over medium-low heat, stirring constantly, until mixture is just bubbly.
4. Arrange cooked broccoli in ramekins or on serving plates; spoon hot egg mixture over broccoli and garnish with reserved egg slices. Serve hot.

Egg Foo Yung Pancakes with Hot Soyed Sauce

Serves 4

6 eggs, beaten
1 tablespoon instant minced onion
2 tablespoons peanut oil
1 can (4½ ounces) shrimp
1 can (3 ounces) chopped mushrooms, drained

2 cups drained bean sprouts
2 tablespoons water chestnuts,
  chopped
¼ teaspoon salt
Hot Soyed Sauce

1. Combine eggs and onion in medium-size bowl; let stand 10 minutes.
2. Heat oil in large skillet or electric fry pan set at 300° F. Drain shrimp, rinsing if label directs; stir shrimp, mushrooms, bean sprouts, water chestnuts and salt into egg mixture.
3. For each pancake, pour about ¼ cup of egg mixture into skillet; fry until golden brown on both sides. Serve with Hot Soyed Sauce.

Hot Soyed Sauce

1 chicken bouillon cube
1 cup boiling water
1 tablespoon cornstarch

1 tablespoon soy sauce
1 tablespoon sherry
1 teaspoon sugar

1. In small saucepan, dissolve bouillon cube in boiling water.
2. Mix cornstarch with soy sauce, sherry and sugar; stir into bouillon and cook over medium-high heat, stirring constantly, until mixture comes to a boil.
3. Continue to cook until sauce is clear and thickened. Keep hot until serving time.

Oriental Eggs Supreme

Serves 6

1 can (10¾ ounces) condensed cream of mushroom soup, undiluted
1 can (4 ounces) sliced mushrooms, undrained
1 can (6 ounces) water chestnuts, drained and sliced
1 can (16 ounces) bean sprouts, drained
1 cup shredded Cheddar cheese
½ cup green pepper, thinly sliced
¼ cup pimiento, chopped
2 tablespoons soy sauce
1 teaspoon instant minced onion
9 hard-cooked eggs, coarsely chopped
chow mein noodles or hot cooked rice

1. Blend soup with mushrooms, including liquid, in large saucepan.
2. Add remaining ingredients except eggs and noodles; cook over medium heat, stirring constantly, until cheese is melted.
3. Gently stir in eggs; bring to serving temperature.
4. Serve hot over noodles with additional soy sauce, if desired.

Fried Rice Quiche

Serves 6

1 (9-inch) pie shell, unbaked
6 eggs, beaten
2 tablespoons butter or margarine
1 cup cooked rice
½ cup green pepper, chopped
½ cup cooked ham, chopped
2 teaspoons soy sauce
1 teaspoon ground ginger
¾ teaspoon garlic salt
1 cup milk
1 tablespoon instant minced onion
⅛ teaspoon pepper

1. Brush pie shell with small amount of beaten eggs; pierce bottom and sides with fork.
2. Bake shell as follows: If using metal pie pan, bake shell in preheated 450° F. oven until golden brown, about 5 minutes. If using pie plate, bake shell at 425° F.
3. Cool on wire rack.
4. Reduce oven temperature to 375° F. for metal pan or 350° F. for pie plate.
5. Melt butter in large skillet; add rice, green pepper, ham, soy sauce, ½ teaspoon ginger and ¼ teaspoon garlic salt.
6. Cook over medium heat, stirring frequently, until rice is golden, about 10 minutes.
7. Sprinkle rice mixture into pie shell.
8. Beat together eggs, milk, onions, pepper, remaining ginger and garlic salt; pour into pie shell and bake in preheated oven until knife inserted halfway between center and outside edge comes out clean, 35 to 40 minutes.
9. Let stand 10 minutes before serving.

NOTE: You may use a frozen deep-dish style pie shell. Thaw shell and pre-bake in preheated 450° F. oven 5 minutes. Bake filled quiche at 350° F.

Haw Jing Tau Tha
(Egg-Shrimp Scramble)

Serves 2

½ cup cooked shrimp, diced
¼ cup scallions, chopped
1 tablespoon peanut oil

4 eggs
1 tablespoon sherry
½ teaspoon salt or sea salt

1. Cook shrimp and scallions in oil in moderately hot skillet until lightly browned.
2. Mix eggs, sherry and salt; pour over shrimp and scallions and cook over medium heat, stirring occasionally to scramble.
3. Cook until eggs are set, but still moist.

Egg Foo Yung with Chinese Brown Gravy

Serves 6

6 eggs, well beaten
1 can (1 pound) bean sprouts, well drained
1 cup cooked veal, pork, beef, chicken, turkey, tuna, shrimp, lobster or crabmeat, chopped

hot cooked rice

1 small onion, peeled and and chopped
½ teaspoon salt
⅛ teaspoon pepper
1 teaspoon butter
Chinese Brown Gravy

1. Combine eggs, bean sprouts, meat or seafood, onion, salt and pepper; mix together lightly.
2. Melt butter in 6-inch skillet; pour ½ cup of egg mixture into skillet. Cook until set and brown on edges; turn and brown other side.
3. Place on hot plate and keep covered until all omelets are cooked.
4. Cover each serving with 2 to 3 tablespoons Chinese Brown Gravy; serve with cooked rice.

Chinese Brown Gravy

Makes 2 cups

6 tablespoons drippings from roast beef, ham or chicken
6 tablespoons flour
2 tablespoons soy sauce

1 teaspoon salt
dash pepper
½ cup cold water
1½ cups hot water

1. Melt fat; blend in flour.
2. Add soy sauce, seasonings and cold water; stir in hot water and cook until smooth and thickened, stirring constantly.
3. Serve with Egg Foo Yung, cooked or fried rice, potatoes, egg noodles, chops, roast beef, pork or veal.

NOTE: Egg Foo Yung is a wonderfully economical dish, for it can be made from either leftovers or staple ingredients from the pantry shelf! Use pork gravy mix if no meat drippings are available. Dilute with soy sauce, water or chicken stock to add flavor.

Lobster Omelet

Serves 4

¾ cup cooked lobster meat, diced
½ cup celery, sliced
¼ cup bamboo shoots, thinly sliced
¼ cup water chestnuts, thinly sliced

2 tablespoons cooked mushrooms, thinly sliced
½ teaspoon salt
⅛ teaspoon pepper
2 tablespoons peanut oil
6 eggs, well beaten

1. Combine all ingredients except peanut oil and eggs.
2. When ready to cook, heat 1½ teaspoons peanut oil in 6-inch skillet.
3. Add eggs to combined ingredients; pour ¼ of mixture into skillet.
4. When brown on one side, flip and brown other side.
5. Remove to heated serving platter.
6. Repeat with remaining oil and egg mixture; serve at once.

Cha Tom

(Indo-China Pork-Seafood Omelet)

Serves 8

½ pound lean raw boneless pork
3 tablespoons peanut oil
½ cup scallions, chopped
⅛ teaspoon cayenne
⅓ cup chicken stock
1 cup chopped cooked shrimp
1 cup fresh mushrooms, sliced

1 teaspoon dried basil (less, if desired)
2 teaspoons fresh mint, chopped
¼ teaspoon ground sage
¼ teaspoon freshly ground pepper
salt to taste
2 dozen oysters, shucked
8 eggs, beaten

1. Fry pork in 1 tablespoon oil with scallions and cayenne until meat begins to turn light.
2. Add chicken stock; cover and simmer gently 20 minutes.
3. Push meat to one side of pan; add shrimp, mushrooms, basil, mint, sage, pepper and salt; cook gently 5 minutes.
4. Add oysters and cook 3 minutes longer, stirring; cool.
5. Heat remaining oil in another skillet.
6. Mix eggs with pork-seafood mixture; divide into 4 portions.
7. Pour one portion of batter into hot oil in skillet to make large pancake; turn to cook on reverse side.
8. Repeat, making 4 large pancakes in all.

NOTE: A good accompaniment to plain steamed rice and soy sauce.

Siamese Stuffed Omelet

Serves 4

1 large clove garlic, crushed
2 tablespoons vegetable oil
½ pound lean ground pork
20 roasted peanuts, ground
½ cup onions, minced

2 teaspoons sugar
¾ teaspoon salt
freshly ground black pepper
  to taste
6 eggs, well beaten

1. Sauté garlic in 1 tablespoon of oil.
2. Add pork and peanuts; fry until pork begins to turn light.
3. Add onions, sugar, salt and pepper, stirring to blend; set aside in warm place.
4. Divide beaten eggs in half, frying one portion at a time in heated remaining oil; repeat making second pancake.
5. Divide filling between the pancakes, placing filling on one-half of each pancake. Fold over once to cover filling and arrange on heated platter.

NOTE: A good luncheon dish!

Salmon Foo Yung with Clear Sauce

Serves 3 to 4

1 can (7¾ ounces) salmon
4 eggs
½ teaspoon salt
1 cup bean sprouts
3 tablespoons scallions, minced

1 can (2 ounces) sliced
  mushrooms, drained
corn oil
Clear Sauce

1. Drain and flake salmon, reserving 1 tablespoon salmon liquid.
2. Beat eggs with salt and reserve salmon liquid; fold in bean sprouts, scallions and mushrooms.
3. Heat enough oil in skillet to cover bottom; spoon 3 tablespoons salmon-egg mixture into hot oil to form a pattie. When bottom is cooked, gently turn and brown other side.
4. Repeat with rest of mixture, adding oil if needed.
5. Serve with Clear Sauce.

Clear Sauce

2 teaspoons cornstarch
1 teaspoon sugar
¾ cup water

⅛ teaspoon salt
1 tablespoon soy sauce

1. Combine cornstarch, sugar, salt, soy sauce and water.
2. Cook, stirring constantly, until thickened and smooth.

85

Green Beans Mandarin

Serves 4 to 6

1½ pounds green beans, cut in
  1-inch pieces (blanched in hot
  water 1 minute)

1 small can mandarin oranges
⅓ tablespoon butter
½ teaspoon ground ginger

1. Combine all ingredients.
2. Heat and serve.

Oriental Celery-Mushroom Sauté

Serves 4

2 tablespoons butter
2 cups celery, diagonally sliced
1 can (4 ounces) sliced mushrooms, drained

½ cup scallions, diagonally sliced
1 can (5 ounces) water chestnuts,
  drained and sliced
1 teaspoon seasoned salt

¼ teaspoon seasoned pepper

1. Melt butter in skillet.
2. Add remaining ingredients; sauté 2 minutes until crisp-tender, stirring constantly.

Bok Choy, Bamboo Shoots & Mushrooms

Serves 4

2 dried Chinese mushrooms
2 medium heads bok choy (Chinese
  greens), about 2 pounds

2 cups bamboo shoots, sliced
Soy-Vinegar Dressing

1. Soften mushrooms in hot water to cover, about 20 minutes; drain. Cut each
   into 4 pieces, discarding woody stems.
2. Wash bok choy (do not dry); cut into 1-inch pieces.
3. Place bok choy in steamer; top with mushrooms and bamboo shoots.
4. Cover and cook 10 minutes, or until vegetables are hot and tender; toss with
   Soy-Vinegar Dressing.

Soy-Vinegar Dressing

1 chicken bouillon cube dissolved in ½ cup hot water
4 tablespoons soy sauce

4 tablespoons rice vinegar
1 tablespoon fresh ginger, shredded
2 teaspoons sugar

4 tablespoons corn or peanut oil

1. Combine bouillon, water, soy sauce, vinegar, ginger and sugar; whisk in oil until
   well blended.
2. Toss with prepared vegetables.

Sweet & Sour Beets with Toasted Almonds

Serves 4 to 6

¼ cup whole blanched almonds
1 can (1 pound) whole beets
¼ teaspoon salt

6 tablespoons apple jelly
1 tablespoon cider vinegar

1. Beforehand, warm almonds in shallow pan in 350° F. oven; while warm, split into halves with tip of knife. Return to oven and toast until light golden-brown color.
2. Drain beets; set aside.
3. Heat jelly, vinegar and salt in saucepan, stirring to blend.
4. Add beets and heat through.
5. Turn into serving dish and sprinkle with almonds.

Carrots de Chine

Serves 4

8 carrots, peeled and grated
¼ cup scallions, diced
scant 3 tablespoons corn oil
¾ cup boiling water
½ teaspoon salt

¼ teaspoon freshly ground black pepper
1 tablespoon tamari sauce (Japanese soy sauce available at health food shop)

1. Sauté carrots and scallions in oil until tender.
2. Add remining ingredients, stirring well; cover and steam just until heated, about 1 minute.

Chinese Cauliflower with Almonds

Serves 4

2 tablespoons corn oil
¼ cup natural almonds, sliced
2 tablespoons butter
1 medium cauliflower, cut into flowerets and sliced ½ inch thick

water
¾ teaspoon salt
2 teaspoons cornstarch

1. Heat 1 tablespoon oil in skillet; add almonds and roast until golden. Remove from pan and set aside.
2. Add remaining oil, butter and cauliflower to pan; cook, stirring, over medium-high heat 3 minutes.
3. Add ½ cup water and salt; cover and simmer 5 minutes.
4. Mix cornstarch with 1 tablespoon water; stir into cauliflower. Cook, stirring, until thickened.
5. Turn into serving dish; sprinkle with roasted almonds.

Stir-Fried Chinese Cabbage

Serves 4

1 medium Chinese cabbage (found in many supermarkets or Oriental food shops)
2 tablespoons peanut oil

pinch sugar
2 tablespoons sherry or sake
1 teaspoon soy sauce
1 teaspoon salt
3 tablespoons chicken broth

1. Cut off leafy end of cabbage; chop coarsely. Slice white part in 1-inch rounds.
2. Heat oil in wok or skillet; stir-fry white part 2 minutes.
3. Add green part; stir-fry over high heat 1 minute longer.
4. Add sugar, sherry, soy sauce, salt and broth; toss lightly to mix. Cover and simmer about 1 minute. Serve immediately.

Microwaved Celery & Peppers, Chinese Style

Serves 4

3 cups celery, diagonally sliced
1 green pepper, cut in short strips
1 tablespoon corn oil

soy sauce
¼ teaspoon salt (optional)
¼ cup slivered almonds, plain or toasted

1. Combine celery, green pepper and oil in 1½-quart microwave-proof casserole.
2. Microwave, covered, on HIGH about 5 minutes, or until steaming.
3. Stir quickly; cover again and let stand 5 minutes.
4. Stir in soy sauce to taste, salt (if desired) and almonds.

Stir-Fried Chinese Pea Pods
with Water Chestnuts

Serves 6

1 tablespoon peanut or corn oil
½ pound Chinese pea pods, cut in half lengthwise
1 small can water chestnuts, drained, sliced and slivered

3 dried Chinese mushrooms, soaked in warm water 15 minutes, drained and sliced
2 to 3 tablespoons chicken broth
soy sauce to taste
minced scallions (optional garnish)

1. Heat oil in wok over high heat.
2. Add remaining ingredients; stir-fry over high heat about 2 to 3 minutes.
3. If desired, garnish with minced scallions.

NOTE: Great served with shrimp fried rice!

Chinese Vegetables

Serves 4

2 cups celery, diagonally sliced
1 cup scallions, diagonally sliced
2 tablespoons corn oil
1 can (10¾ ounces) chicken broth
½ cup water

1 can (16 ounces) Chinese
  vegetables, drained
3 tablespoons cornstarch
2 tablespoons soy sauce
hot cooked rice

1. Cook celery and scallions in oil in skillet until just tender.
2. Add remaining ingredients except rice; cook, stirring, until thickened.
3. Serve over rice with additional soy sauce.

Curried Eggplant Raita

Makes 3 cups

1 medium-size eggplant, weighing
  about 1 pound
1 teaspoon salt
1 teaspoon sesame seeds
½ teaspoon ground coriander

1 tablespoon corn oil
1 tablespoon fresh lemon juice
1 small onion, peeled and minced
1 cup plain yogurt
1 large tomato, peeled and diced

1. Wash eggplant; slash skin with knife to allow steam to escape.
2. Bake on foil-lined pan in preheated 350° F. oven until soft, about 45 minutes; allow to cool.
3. Scoop out pulp and mash.
4. Combine seasonings, oil, lemon juice and onion with yogurt; blend with eggplant.
5. Stir in tomato; chill thoroughly.

NOTE: This is a delightful Indian vegetarian dish. Great to serve in summer!

Vegetarian Sukiyaki

Serves 4 to 6

2 cups tofu, shredded
2 tablespoons corn oil
½ cup green pepper,
  thinly sliced
1 cup celery, sliced
1 cup bean sprouts
½ cup scallions, sliced

1 cup Chinese cabbage, cut in
  1½-inch strips
1 small can (3 ounces) mushrooms
2 tablespoons soy sauce
1 tablespoon honey
handful cleaned spinach
brown rice

1. Brown tofu in corn oil; add remaining ingredients except spinach.
2. Cover and cook over low heat 12 minutes.
3. A few minutes before serving, add spinach. Serve with brown rice.

Curried Vegetable Melange

Serves 6

1 cup water
1 chicken bouillon cube
8 ounces fresh broccoli spears
   (½ medium bunch)
8 ounces fresh cauliflowerets
   (about 1½ cups)

¼ pound fresh mushrooms, quartered
¼ cup plain yogurt
¼ cup low-sugar apricot spread
½ teaspoon fresh lemon juice
¼ teaspoon curry powder
⅛ teaspoon salt

1. Combine water and bouillon cube in large saucepan; heat until cube disappears.
2. Add broccoli, cauliflower and mushrooms; cover and cook until broccoli is tender-crisp, about 5 minutes. Drain.
3. Combine remaining ingredients in small saucepan; cook and stir until sauce is heated to serving temperature. Pour over vegetables.

NOTE: Try this sauce cold as a fruit dip. Just stir together sauce ingredients and refrigerate. It's especially delicious with banana slices!

Zen Vegetarian Loaf

Serves 3 to 4

1 medium eggplant, peeled and
   chopped
1 cup celery, diced
1 medium onion, chopped
1 carrot, grated
1 tomato, diced
4 tablespoons butter
1 egg, beaten
1 cup cooked brown rice

½ teaspoon dried oregano
1 tablespoon wheat germ
1 tablespoon tofu (soybean curd,
   available at Oriental or health
   food shops)
1 clove garlic, crushed
sea salt to taste
handful sesame seeds (optional
   garnish)

1. Sauté vegetables in butter a few minutes over low heat, stirring until vegetables begin to become limp; cool.
2. Add beaten egg, brown rice, oregano, wheat germ, tofu, garlic and sea salt; mix well.
3. Form into loaf in greased baking dish; garnish with toasted sesame seeds, if desired.
4. Bake in preheated 350° F. oven about 30 minutes.

Fresh Fruit & Lychee Compote

Serves 6 to 8

1 honeydew melon, scooped in
  small balls
2 oranges, peeled and cut in
  segments
1 apple diced

1 or 2 cans (8 ounces each)
  lychees in syrup
1 pint strawberries, hulled
½ cup sugar, or to taste
¼ cup port wine

dash fresh lemon juice (optional)

1. Combine melon balls, oranges, apple, undrained lychees, strawberries and sugar in bowl.
2. Toss with wine and lemon juice, if desired.
3. Cover and chill 2 to 3 hours.
4. Toss gently before serving; serve in stemmed goblets or sherbet dishes.

Chinese Pineapple Steamed Sponge Cake

Makes 8-inch cake

1 can (8¼ ounces) sliced pineapple in syrup
5 eggs, separated, at room
  temperature
¾ cup packed brown sugar

1 teaspoon pure vanilla extract
1¼ cups sifted all-purpose flour
1 tablespoon cornstarch
pinch salt
about 2 cups water

1. Drain pineapple, reserving ¼ cup syrup; pat pineapple slices dry on paper towel.
2. Line bottom of 8-inch spring-form pan with waxed paper; arrange pineapple slices on bottom.
3. Beat egg yolks with pineapple syrup, sugar and vanilla on high speed of electric mixer, about 5 minutes, until light and fluffy.
4. Slowly mix in flour, cornstarch and salt.
5. Beat egg whites until stiff peaks form.
6. Fold half the egg whites into batter with wire whisk. (Batter will be quite stiff.)
7. Fold in remaining egg whites until thoroughly blended.
8. Pour into prepared pan; tap pan on counter to remove air bubbles. Cover with foil, forming a slight dome to allow cake to rise.
9. Bring water to a boil in wok. Elevate cake above water with steamer rack or over-turned bowl; cover and steam 35 minutes, or until cake tests done. (Add more water, if necessary.)
10. Turn cake upside down on cake rack; let cool before removing from pan. Peel off waxed paper and cut with serrated knife.

Pineapple Rice Pudding

Serves 6 to 8

3 cups cooked rice	3 eggs, separated
3 cups milk	1 can (15¼ ounces) crushed
¼ cup sugar	pineapple
1 tablespoon butter or margarine	1 teaspoon ground cinnamon
½ teaspoon salt	½ cup flaked coconut

1. Combine rice, milk, sugar, butter and salt in saucepan; cook over medium heat, stirring occasionally, until thick and creamy; about 25 minutes.
2. Beat egg yolks; blend a little creamed rice into the yolks.
3. Stir yolk mixture into creamed rice; cook 1 minute longer.
4. Remove from heat, add pineapple and cinnamon, and cool.
5. Beat egg whites until stiff but not dry; fold into cooled rice.
6. Turn into greased 9-inch square baking pan, top with coconut, and bake in preheated 325° F. oven for 25 minutes.

Ceylonese Love Cake

Makes 10-inch cake

6 egg yolks	1½ cups sifted cake flour
¼ cup water	½ teaspoon cinnamon
2 tablespoons honey	½ teaspoon cardamon
2 tablespoons rosewater	¼ teaspoon nutmeg
1½ cups sugar	¼ teaspoon salt
1 teaspoon brandy	6 egg whites
½ teaspoon pure vanilla extract	¾ teaspoon cream of tartar
½ cup cashew nuts, finely chopped	

1. Beat egg yolks until thick and lemon-colored.
2. Gradually add water, honey and rosewater; continue beating until very thick.
3. Add sugar, 2 tablespoons at a time, beating well after each addition; blend in brandy and vanilla.
4. Sift together flour, cinnamon, cardamon, nutmeg and salt; sift 2 more times.
5. Divide spice-flour mixture into 4 parts; add one part at a time to yolk mixture, beating well after each addition.
6. Beat egg whites until foamy; add cream of tartar and beat until moist, glossy peaks form.
7. Gently fold whites and chopped nuts into yolk mixture.
8. Bake in ungreased 10-inch tube pan in preheated 325° F. oven 65 to 70 minutes.
9. Invert pan; cool at least 1 hour.

NOTE: This is a delicious lighter version than the traditional flat, crusty love cake made with semolina.

Honey Almond Pears

Serves 6

3 fresh California Bartlett pears
fresh lemon juice
⅓ cup sugar
2 tablespoons honey

2 tablespoons margarine or butter
1 tablespoon milk
⅔ cup natural, unblanched almonds, sliced

1. Pare, halve, and core pears; coat with lemon juice. Place, rounded-side up, in 10-inch pie plate or baking dish.
2. Combine sugar, honey, margarine and milk in small saucepan; boil for 4 minutes, stirring to prevent burning.
3. Mix in almonds and pour over pears; bake at 350° F. for 15 minutes.
4. Serve hot or cold as a dessert or meat accompaniment.

Chinese Almond Cookies

Makes about 3 dozen cookies

½ cup raw whole almonds
1½ cups all-purpose flour
½ teaspoon baking powder
¼ teaspoon salt

½ cup butter or margarine
⅓ cup sugar
½ teaspoon almond extract
1 tablespoon gin or vodka or water

1. Reserve 36 whole almonds; finely chop or grind remainder.
2. Sift flour with baking powder and salt.
3. Thoroughly cream butter with sugar.
4. Stir in all remaining ingredients except whole almonds; form dough into 36 balls.
5. Place on greased cookie sheets; press a whole almond into center of each ball.
6. Bake in preheated 350° F. oven 20 minutes, or until light brown.

Oriental Almond Rice Cookies

Makes 2 dozen cookies

½ cup corn oil
½ cup brown sugar
1 egg
1 teaspoon pure almond extract
¾ cup rye flour

pinch salt
1 teaspoon baking powder
2 tablespoons soy flour
¾ cup rice flour

1. Beat together oil, sugar, egg and almond extract in large mixing bowl.
2. Add remaining ingredients; mix well.
3. Shape dough into 1-inch balls; place on cookie sheet about 3 inches apart and flatten with fork to about ¼ inch thick.
4. Bake in preheated 350° F. oven for 10 to 12 minutes, or golden brown.

NOTE: Soy, rice and rye flours are available in health food stores.

Korean Date Balls

Serves 6

30 dates
2 tablespoons sugar

1 teaspoon ground cinnamon
3 tablespoons pine nuts, finely chopped

1. Seed dates and steam for 15 minutes: purée dates or press through a very coarse strainer.
2. Add sugar and cinnamon: mix well.
3. Shape into ½-inch balls and roll in pine nuts. Arrange attractively on small plates.

Peking Dust

Serves 8

3 egg whites
¼ teaspoon cream of tartar
1¼ cups plus 3 tablespoons sugar
1 cup pecan halves
2 cups water

1 cup peanut oil
1 can (10 ounces) chestnuts
2 tablespoons light brown sugar
1½ cups heavy cream
¾ teaspoon vanilla extract

1. Combine egg whites and cream of tartar in small mixing bowl: beat until foamy.
2. Gradually add ¾ cup sugar: continue beating until stiff and glossy.
3. Using ⅓ cup mixture for each shell, form meringue into 8 individual shells on a baking sheet lined with brown paper: bake at 250° F. for 50 minutes.
4. Turn off oven: leave shells in oven 1 hour longer.
5. Combine pecans and water in saucepan: bring to a boil. Reduce heat, simmer 1 minute, then drain.
6. Add ½ cup sugar, stirring until pecans are well coated.
7. Turn out onto baking sheet lined with waxed paper: let dry 30 minutes.
8. Heat oil in wok or large skillet to 375° F.: add half the pecans and cook 1 to 2 minutes, stirring frequently until sugar forms a glaze.
9. Remove pecans from oil and spread out on oiled platter: repeat with remaining pecans and set aside.
10. Drain chestnuts, reserving ¼ cup liquid.
11. Combine chestnuts, reserved chestnut liquid and brown sugar in saucepan: bring to a boil.
12. Reduce heat: simmer 10 to 15 minutes until thickened and pasty.
13. Cool to room temperature, then purée chestnut mixture in food mill.
14. Combine heavy cream, remaining 3 tablespoons sugar and vanilla extract: whip until stiff.
15. Gently fold chestnut purée into whipped cream: spoon into meringue shells and garnish with glazed pecans.

Banana Fritters

Serves 6

1 egg, separated
⅓ cup water
1 teaspoon melted butter
½ cup unsifted all-purpose flour

dash salt
dash ground cinnamon
2 teaspoons sugar
peanut oil

4 firm bananas

1. With rotary beater, beat egg yolk, water and butter together in a bowl.
2. Combine dry ingredients and mix well to blend thoroughly; stir into egg mixture.
3. Cover and refrigerate 2 hours.
4. Heat oil to 370° F.
5. Beat egg white until stiff; beat into batter.
6. Peel bananas and cut diagonally in 1-inch slices.
7. Dip banana pieces into batter; fry until golden on all sides.
8. Drain on absorbent paper; serve warm.

Cantonese Apricot Bars

Makes 30 bars

¼ cup butter or margarine
¼ cup shortening
1½ cups light brown sugar, packed
1 cup all-purpose flour
¼ teaspoon ground ginger
2 eggs

½ teaspoon salt
1 teaspoon lemon peel, grated
2 tablespoons fresh lemon juice
1 can (4 ounces) shredded coconut, toasted
1 cup dried apricots, diced
½ cup blanched slivered almonds

1. To form bottom layer, beat butter, shortening and ½ cup brown sugar together until well mixed.
2. Blend in flour and ⅛ teaspoon ground ginger.
3. Pat into greased 13 x 9-inch baking pan; bake in preheated 350° F. oven 10 minutes.
4. Let stand a few minutes, then spread with topping.
5. To prepare topping, beat together eggs, remaining brown sugar, remaining ginger, salt, lemon peel and juice.
6. Stir in coconut, apricots and almonds.
7. Spread topping over bottom layer; return to oven and bake 25 minutes longer, or until topping is golden brown.
8. Cool and cut into bars.

NOTE: To toast coconut, spread in shallow pan and bake in 350° F. oven about 10 minutes, or until golden brown. Stir frequently.

Chinese Fried Pastries with Walnut Filling

Makes 16 pastries

¾ cup dates, chopped
¼ cup water
¼ cup sugar
dash salt
¾ cup walnuts, chopped

1 can (8 ounces) refrigerated
 crescent dinner rolls
1 egg yolk
1 teaspoon water
2 teaspoons sesame seeds

fat for deep-fat frying

1. Combine dates, water, sugar and salt; simmer until thick, stirring frequently.
2. Cook and stir in walnuts.
3. Open package of rolls and unroll half carefully, without separating at perforations.
4. On lightly floured board, place one rectangle of dough over the other, reversing angles of perforations.
5. Roll dough to a very thin 7 x 17-inch rectangle. Cut in halves, then cut each piece into four 3½-inch squares.
6. Place a rounded teaspoon of walnut filling on each square; moisten edges of dough and press together over filling, turning points in slightly to crescents.
7. Repeat with second half of dough and filling.
8. Beat egg yolk lightly with water; brush over pastries and sprinkle with sesame seeds.
9. Heat fat to 360° F.; fry pastries, a few at a time, for about 4 minutes, turning frequently.
10. Drain on paper towels; serve warm.

Apricot Shangri-la Pudding

Serves 6

2 tablespoons light brown sugar
1 can (16 ounces) apricot halves,
 undrained
1¼ cups unsifted all-purpose flour
2 teaspoons baking powder
¾ cup sugar
¼ teaspoon ground ginger
¼ teaspoon salt

¼ cup butter or margarine, melted
2 eggs
⅓ cup milk
1 teaspoon lemon peel, grated
⅓ cup flaked coconut
1 cup heavy cream, whipped and
 sweetened

1. Sprinkle brown sugar over bottom of greased 9-inch cake pan.
2. Pour 2 tablespoons of apricot syrup over bottom of pan; drain apricot halves and arrange in pan. Set aside.
3. Sift together flour, baking powder, sugar, ginger and salt.
4. In large bowl, beat butter with eggs, milk and lemon peel; add dry ingredients, stirring until smooth.
5. Pour batter over apricots in pan. Place baking pan in another large pan; add hot water to reach halfway up side of baking pan. Bake at 350° F. for 50 minutes.
6. Remove cake pan from water; invert immediately onto serving plate.
7. Sprinkle coconut in border around top of pudding; serve warm with whipped cream.